My Cat Won't Bark!

(A Relationship Epiphany)

Kevin Darné

About the Author

Kevin Darné is the President & CEO of Conation Enterprises; a company that helps people facilitate change within in order to bring about change without. Kevin is also a Chicago dating advice examiner for Examiner. com, providing advice and guidance in the tricky world of dating. He also contributes articles and blogs to Hubpages and Yahoo Shine. The primary message within his articles is one of self-empowerment. For additional information visit www.lovealert911.com

ISBN: 1468104721
ISBN 13: 9781468104721

Library of Congress Control Number: 2011963373
CreateSpace, North Charleston, SC

My Cat Won't Bark! is about seeing things as they are in our relationships.

We must ask ourselves to strip away any illusions we may have conjured up and remove unrealistic expectations. For example, we all know it's unrealistic to expect a liar to be honest, a thief to be trustworthy, a cheater to be loyal, an apple to taste like a banana, or a cat to bark! Can people change? Certainly. But can you change someone? Absolutely not! Change comes from within and can only happen when an individual decides *they* want to change. All we can do is ask; it's the other person's choice to appease us or not.

Once someone we're in relationship with has indicated by words or deeds they have no intention of fulfilling our desires we have a decision to make. Is not getting something we want a "deal breaker"? If it is, get out. If it's not, learn to live without. Efforts we make to change a partner generally lead to frustration on our part and resentment on our mate's part.

Our lives are the result of decisions and choices we've made along the way.

We select our own friends, lovers, and spouses. No matter what has taken place, we cannot escape the fact that at some point in time we said yes to this person. Ultimately we are responsible for our own happiness in life. When we choose to forget we made the decision to enter into a

Kevin Darné

relationship, we negate a very important truth: we have the power to make better choices and decisions for ourselves in the future! Knowing we have options is empowering. Ideally, with time and life experience, we gain wisdom that helps us make better decisions in our lives.

The philosophy behind *My Cat Won't Bark!* centers on the value of learning to make relationship decisions with awareness and to stop living life on autopilot. Once we acknowledge our cat won't bark, it's important we assume responsibility for our past decisions and strive to make wiser decisions in the future. It's also essential that we learn to either embrace our reality or be willing to change it. The choice is ours.

I've been in every type of relationship a man and a woman can have. I've had girlfriends, booty calls, friends with benefits, and numerous one-night stands. I've lived with several women and have been married twice. After all this, I had a "relationship epiphany."

There was only one common denominator in all of those relationships: me. In fact, when I looked back, I realized I spent more time and effort on selecting a vacation destination—reserving the airline transportation and a nonsmoking hotel room with a king bed, on a high floor and away from the elevators, at a hotel or resort with various other amenities, daily excursions, and nightly entertainment—than I did in selecting a mate!

My relationships came about through happenstance. One thing led to another whatever, however, and whenever. The only real effort I made was trying to make the most out of a situation. Sure I had a few *guidelines* but nothing nearly as specific as my vacation requirements.

My perspective was that too much thinking about a prospective mate's potential seemed unromantic and time consuming. There's a well-known proverb that says, "He who fails to plan, plans to fail." That was me. When it came to love and romance, I was shopping without a list. "I'll know it when I see it" was my mantra of the day. In fact, I'd never taken the time to create a list of traits I wanted and needed in a mate. They were loosely in the back of my mind. Naturally, this strategy often led to frustration and disappointment.

I'd bought into the myth that relationships required a lot of work, and this led me to stay in some relationships for far too long. I now know the problem was not so much with my mates as it was my selecting them to begin with. If you want an apple but purchase an onion instead, whose fault is that? The real work is in selecting the right mate! You can't select the right mate until you really know yourself and have formed your personal life philosophy. That takes time! After you have selected the "right" mate for yourself, much of what might be considered work actually becomes a labor of love.

I won't promise you this book will change your life. That's entirely up to you. In my own life, I've come to realize there is a big difference in knowing what to do and doing it. On the surface, much of the book appears to be common sense, but as one of my friends once told me, "Common sense is not so common anymore."

Kevin Darné

Sometimes seeing a situation through another person's eyes helps to crystallize what we have suspected to be true. There are other times when hearing another person's opinion creates an "epiphany moment" in our lives, clearing the way for us to make a decision that we have been putting off. There are no fancy degrees hanging on my office walls from various distinguished universities, and I do not have published scientific studies backing the opinions stated in this book.

The following pages came as a result of what took me decades to learn through trial and error. In fact, I will go on record here and now to tell you I'm still learning! Life, after all, is a work in progress, and you don't graduate until you die. The world may not owe you anything, but you owe yourself the world!

It's your life. Take the wheel!

Contents

Introduction

Mary awakened one bright Saturday morning with a massive craving for cereal and a banana. She descended the stairs and entered her kitchen to find her fruit basket contained only an apple. Mary held the apple lovingly in her hands speaking softly to it, "I wish you were a banana and not an apple." She closed her eyes and pictured herself holding a banana; she imagined the smell of it, the sweet taste of it, and how much she loved it in her cereal. Mary opened her eyes and saw she was still holding an apple.

Frustration, resentment, and anger began to set in. Mary imagined all the other households on her block had bananas in them while she was stuck with an apple. She slammed the apple against her kitchen counter and started cursing at it. She jumped up and down, pulled her hair out, and beat her head against the wall until she passed out.

Mary came to a few minutes later only to see she still had an apple. She began to cry uncontrollably until she fell asleep on the kitchen floor. When Mary awoke this time, she felt an immense sense of clarity. She realized her apple was always going to be an apple. Her options were to make do with what she had, slice up the apple, and eat it with her cereal or leave the house and go shopping for a banana. Countless times each and every day, this scenario is played out across the country, only instead of fruit, it's our mates, significant others, or spouses that we want to change.

The moment of clarity, or the realization that *My Cat Won't Bark*, puts us at a crossroad. It's a reality check, prompting a decision to either accept what is or walk away to start anew. Both options can lead to happiness and peace of mind.

Seeing things as they are is such a simple concept, but it's hard to put into practice for ourselves. Generally speaking, we consider ourselves experts at solving someone else's life problems. We know exactly what needs to be done and are more than willing to tell them the best way to approach their problems. However, when the onus is on us to either accept things as they really are or move on, we come up with countless reasons or justifications for keeping the status quo.

One popular excuse is "We have kids." But as Dr. Phil is fond of saying, "Kids would rather be from a broken home than live in a broken home." Raising children in a house full of tension is not doing them any favors. "It would be too financially devastating to break up" is another common reason people give for staying in unhealthy relationships. How much is your peace of mind, body, and soul worth to you? Or they say, "We've been together for ten years." But the only thing worse than being in a bad relationship for ten years is being in it for ten years and a day!

When we choose to stay in an unhappy relationship, we are actually saying "I believe this is the best that I can do." We have a lack of confidence that we can start over and end up with a better life. The longer anyone stays in a negative environment, the easier it is to become cynical about life. We begin to feel powerless when it comes to controlling our own destiny. In fact, if we are not careful, it's easy to magnify our problems to such an extent we behave like a deer in headlights. Life simply washes over us, and the years roll by with nothing to distinguish them until the day we die.

Few people possess true self-love. They are willing to endure circumstances in their own relationships they would never advise their adult children to settle for. Deep down inside, most people do not feel they deserve the best that life has to offer. So they stop seeking better ways to improve their lives. They believe it takes too much effort, and if the result is not what they want, then it has been a waste of time. Nothing could be further from the truth! To truly be alive means having desires, stretching to reach goals, taking risks, dancing in celebration of victory, and recovering from heartaches stronger, wiser, and more determined to get it right. Life is the most precious gift you will ever receive. Every day, hour, and minute that passes by is time you can't get back.

The world may not owe you anything, but you owe yourself the world! You are powerful! Let today be the day you start doing some introspective thinking. Look at the decisions that have brought you to where you are today. Each of us determines who our friends, lovers, and spouses will be. Every choice along the way in your life was met with an option to say yes or no. Placing the blame on others for your lot in life makes you powerless.

The beauty of accepting responsibility for your circumstances is in knowing that if you created them, then it's absolutely possible for you to change them! You have the power to make decisions for a better life. When we change, our circumstances change. The choice is yours to become proactive or remain on autopilot. Let me stress the purpose of this book is to help us determine if we have made a bad choice for ourselves or if we have unrealistic expectations for the person we are with. It's not about establishing who is wrong or is right. There really is no "right" or "wrong" only "agree" and "disagree".

It's about knowing what you want and determining if your mate is right *for you*. Ultimately we are all in search of someone who agrees with us and wants what we want. Should you decide that he or she is not what you want; rest assured there is someone else that is right for you. There are over seven billion people that inhabit our planet!

My Cat Won't Bark! explains a relationship epiphany. It's the process of finding clarity, acknowledging reality, and making informed decisions going forward based upon your true desires. Often what we say we want is not always what we truly want.

The best way to determine if you really want something is by looking at your actions or dedication in pursuing your goal. If I tell you I want to lose thirty pounds but I continue to take in the same amount of calories, fat, and carbohydrates while watching television and avoiding exercise, at some point you'd begin to wonder if I am truly serious about wanting to lose weight. My actions do not coincide with my desires.

Another example is a woman who tells her friends she wants to marry a man who is well educated, earns six figures, is romantic, and enjoys traveling to exotic destinations. However, the men she dates are from the local tavern or the economically depressed section of town. Odds are she is not going to meet her Mr. Right unless he accidentally takes the wrong off-ramp and asks her for directions.

Wants and Needs

One of the reasons we often do not get what we want is because we do not internalize our desires into needs. There are five basic needs required to survive as an adult.

1. Air

2. Water

3. Food

4. Shelter

5. Clothing

All of the above needs are available at any county jail. In other words, it's not too difficult to acquire our *basic needs*.

Beyond the five basic needs are things that fall under the "wants" or "would be nice to have" categories. When people convert a *want* into a *need*, they're almost unstoppable in pursuing the object of their desire. The actions of a drug addict prove this point. An addict with a three-hundred-dollar daily habit will do whatever it takes to fulfill his need. He knows if he fails to get his fix, he'll become sick and suffer severe pain. Three hundred dollars a day multiplied by 365 days a year comes to $109,500 annually! It's human nature for us to find a way to get the things we need despite the cost.

Naturally, it would be impossible to convert our every desire into a need. If we pursued every want with the same urgency as a need, we'd become mentally and physically drained. Fortunately, a lot of the things we want fall under a few headings. For instance, if your goal is to have a large beautiful home, travel the world, own a luxury car, and wear high-fashion clothing, you wouldn't have to convert each of these desires into a need. Converting just one want (money) into a need will provide you with all of the above. There are a couple of options available.

1. You can put all your energy into developing a high-powered career that will generate a substantial income, allowing you to acquire the lifestyle you want.

2. You can set your sights on marrying someone who possesses everything you want and is willing to share his or her world with you.

We'll revisit the techniques that can be used to convert a want into a need in the workbook section of this book.

It is important to first know what you want in a relationship and life in general. If you want something bad enough to convert it into a need, you'll most likely get it. Take a few minutes to make a list of the characteristics you want in a mate and compare it to what you actually have in your mate. If your spouse or mate does not possess these characteristics, it's time you examine how and why you selected someone who did not meet your desires.

It's also possible you already have what you *really* want, and your list is actually filled with things that were instilled in you by society, family, or friends. If this is the case, it's time you destroy that list and stop pretending you want something you really don't want. Not everyone wants the same things or is attracted to the same type of person. It's a cliché, but it's true that there's someone for everyone.

After you have examined your list and determined it contains the things you truly care about, the next step is to find out why you went against your desires when you chose your significant other. It was your choice, and over time you have to learn to adjust or give up unrealistic expectations. As stated in the preface, it's unrealistic to expect liars to be honest, thieves to be trustworthy, cheaters to be loyal, cats to bark, or apples to taste like bananas! In the same way, having unrealistic expectations in relationships leads to frustration and unhappiness.

Are you ready to examine how you ended up with an apple when you wanted a banana?

Wherever the Wind Takes Me

Impulsive Connections

Impulse is the thing marketing and sales organizations wish they could initiate in each of us. You're standing in line at the grocery store, and suddenly you throw a candy bar or gossip magazine into your cart even though neither item was on your list.

It's a totally impulsive move! This is what often happens when we select a mate, just as we know the candy bar will not help us reach our weight goal and the gossip magazine is nothing more than mindless information about people we don't know and most likely will never meet. We still find ourselves indulging for the sake of temporary pleasure. Unfortunately, selecting the wrong mate by impulse can cause much worse damage to your life than eating a candy bar or reading a trash magazine.

Why You May Be With the Wrong Person

Impulse is defined in the dictionary as a sudden inclination to act, usually without premeditation. In other words; it's a decision to do something without weighing the long-term consequences. Most of us have had these "What the hell, why not?" moments in our life. This impulse could be to do something as simple as purchasing a candy bar at the last second as we check out of a grocery store, to call in sick on a beautiful morning, or possibly to go home with a total stranger to have sex after a couple of drinks.

The human brain seems to have two parts, the parent and the child. When we listen to the parent side, we look for clues or warnings and ask questions before making a decision. When we listen to the child side, we ignore anything that might keep us from having what we want at the moment. It's a mental rebellion of sorts. Each time the parent side raises a question, the child side quickly shuts it down with justifications such as "I deserve it," "I want it," or "It'll be fun." Whenever the child side of the brain takes over, it's all about me. We are inconsiderate of other people's feelings. The child wants what it wants when it wants it. This is often the case with people who knowingly enter into or continue sexual relationships with married or attached people. The child side of the brain is selfish and could care less about potential consequences.

Fortunately for most of us, the vast majority of society listens to the parent side of their brain more often than the child side when making decisions. Every decision we make has some bearing on our life, but very few are as important as to whom we allow into our lives as friends, lovers, mates, and spouses. And yet this is the one area where most people are very lax. We do not want to take the time to examine the person we feel an attraction toward. Instead of having a person earn our trust over time, we want to extend them the benefit of the doubt. Often we don't bother to ask some of the obvious questions such as "Are you married?" In fact, we are afraid of turning this person off by asking too many questions. And yet if they were sincerely interested in us, they'd be more than happy to answer all of our questions and ask us many of the same ones in return.

Another thrilling aspect to meeting new people is the mystery of the unknown. It excites us not knowing much about a person early on. We want to discover his or her likes and dislikes over time as if slowly licking ice cream instead of biting through it and chewing.

It's a romantic cliché to say, "We met and one thing led to another," "Nothing was planned," or "It was pure coincidence," but this is sometimes how we make our relationship decisions. It seems totally unromantic to write down the traits you want in a friend, lover, mate, or spouse and then have the discipline to take the time to see if someone we're interested in meets our criteria.

Chemistry Rules the Day!

Chemistry is one of those things we have a difficult time explaining, and yet we all experience it. There is something special about meeting a person who takes our breath away, makes our heart beat faster, or causes us to daydream about them. Laughter comes easily. We get butterflies in our stomach, and we're highly aroused by a single touch or short kiss from this individual, and all the while we barely know a single thing about them!

There are other times we intellectually know enough about a person to realize they are the complete opposite of what we have stated we want and need in a mate, but we refuse to let the opportunity pass us by to explore the exciting feeling we experience whenever they are in the room.

Sometimes we enter into relationships totally blinded by chemistry, and once we learn a few details that otherwise would have alarmed us early on, we feel its okay to overlook them because we have already started down the relationship path. Perhaps sex with this person is mind blowing, or the good feeling you have whenever they are around outweighs any troublesome character flaws he or she might have.

You may even develop a mindset that you are going to "help" this person improve over time. A love-conquers-all mentality takes hold as more time is invested in the relationship. You automatically ignore any red flags pointed out to you by friends and family regarding this person because they don't really know him or her the way you do. In fact, you may even develop an "It's us against the world" attitude as you staunchly defend your mate. This is often the case in abusive relationships.

Accidents Happen!

A connection based on impulse can also lead to an accidental relationship. Case in point: you are certain there is no long-term relationship potential with someone; however, you are so physically attracted to him or her you decide to have a one-night stand, which becomes a regular booty call, which leads to a friends-with-benefits relationship, until one day something tragic or upsetting happens in one of your lives. Either you are there for them or they are there for you in a moment of crisis. You begin to spend more time with one another, and one day one of you suggests moving in together. In almost no time flat, you have gone from having a one-night stand with a hot stranger to being in a full-blown relationship with someone you knew from the outset was not spouse material.

Another example of how an accidental relationship can occur is when a woman accepts an invitation to go out on a date with a man she clearly is not attracted to and has no interest in, but since her calendar is empty, she says to yourself, "What the hell, why not?" After she's had a couple of drinks, his jokes seem funny. He tells her a painful story from his past, and by the end of the evening she decides to lower her standards by having sex with him to make his day. The following day he sends her flowers or a gift, followed up by an invitation to get together again the next weekend.

A part of her wants to burst his bubble, and yet she had a decent time with him and does not want to be cruel.

This man greets her like a puppy dog, eager to please, and pampers her every step of the way as he strokes her ego. Back-to-back weekends together lead to a vacation, and before she knows it she is in a relationship with one type of man while fantasizing about the kind of man she is naturally attracted to.

Over time, it becomes impossible to fake passion and excitement with this person, yet she does not want to be a villain by ending a long-term relationship or marriage with a great person simply because there is no chemistry.

This often happens to people who believe one is better off marrying someone who loves them more than he or she loves them. In many respects, it's only natural to become a little cynical or jaded after having several bad relationships in your pursuit of the ideal romantic partner. We may decide we would rather have a relationship where our mate is madly in love with us while we are not emotionally invested. The following are causes that lead to impulsive connections.

Legitimate and Hallmark Holidays

Although most of us eventually outgrow peer pressure from our friends and associates, we still find ourselves being sucked into depression during the holidays if we are alone. This is especially true on Christmas, New Year's Eve, and Valentine's Day. It's during these particular holidays that there is so much focus placed upon us from advertisers to give our spouses or significant others diamonds, cars, roses, candy, and assorted other gifts in addition to attending parties or taking romantic getaways. Everywhere you go, it seems there are couples of all ages, sizes, and ethnicities holding hands, kissing, laughing, and playfully teasing one another. Often these holidays are used for life-changing events, such as getting engaged. During the holiday season, one may start to believe being with the wrong person is better than having no one.

The Third Wheel Syndrome

There are many single people who suddenly find themselves surrounded by married or attached friends. These friends continue to invite them to various outings, barbeques, parties, movies, and dinners. It's a good-faith effort to show their single friends they have every intention of maintaining a relationship with them. However, over time, the single friend gets tired of being the third or fifth wheel. There always comes a point in the evening where the couple exchanges a knowing glance of love, gives each other a kiss, holds hands, or playfully complains about each other's habits, such as his snoring or her leaving shoes all over the house. All of these gestures serve to remind the single person that they don't even have someone to play with. Eventually one of the attached people will tell the single friend that they know of someone who is also single, and he or she would be perfect for him or her. The couple's intentions are pure. They only want their single friend to experience the joy and happiness they have found. However, blind dates seldom work out. Gradually the single friend pulls away from those in relationships.

Biological Clocks and Accidental Pregnancies

This one applies to women who find their most fertile years are passing them by while they have yet to meet Mr. Right. Some of them decide to have a child with Mr. Right Now. In other instances, it's truly an accidental pregnancy, but the woman realizes there may not be many more opportunities to conceive. She may have given up on the idea of Mr. Right, and so she decides to have the child.

During the first half of the twentieth century, it was very common for a man to marry his pregnant girlfriend prior to the birth of the child. A couple would give it their best shot to make things work for the sake of the child. Society frowned upon unwed couples bringing children into the world. Today pregnancy outside of marriage is so common that we've created titles for our significant other who is a co-parent but not our spouse, such as baby momma and baby daddy.

It's tough enough trying to sustain a relationship with your ideal mate while raising children, but that's nothing compared to having children with someone who just happened to be in your life. Setting goals is a good thing most of the time, but when it comes to getting married or having kids by a certain age; you run the risk of making a major mistake if you try to suit an arbitrary timeframe. When it comes to making a decision about who to have children with, one should strongly consider what's in the child's best interest.

If you have chosen to have sex with someone you would never consider having kids with, it's up to you to take every necessary precaution to avoid an accidental pregnancy. Fortunately we live in an era where there are more birth control methods than ever before. In addition, we now have the morning-after pill, and a woman legally has a right to choose. Given all the options we have today, there still may be the occasional accidental pregnancy, but there is no such thing as accidental birth. The woman is legally the only one in a relationship who has the power to make a man a father. Male readers of this book should keep this in mind. By the same token, a man who wants a child cannot force a woman to have his child.

Hollywood

In the 2009 movie *Up in the Air*, George Clooney's character tries to persuade a would-be groom with cold feet to proceed down the aisle by telling him, "Life is better with company."

Chick flicks keep alive the idea that love conquers all. They suggest that there's someone right around the corner, up the street, across the country, or around the globe that was born to be your soul mate, your lover for life, and your best friend. Hollywood takes things a step further by making sure the men in these movies are rich, handsome, smart, powerful, and well traveled. Considering the influence of these movies, is it any wonder so many of us create laundry lists for potential spouses that are too unrealistic for any one human being to live up to? The list you've created should be much more grounded in reality.

The women in these movies are typically beautiful, with some type of problem to overcome, or there's an issue to resolve that requires a man to sweep her off her feet before they can ride away into the sunset. One recent example of such a movie is Tyler Perry's *Good Deeds*; a rich man rescues a financially strapped single mother who works as a night janitor in his building. You can't blame Hollywood, though. Not many people want to pay ten dollars to watch a mailman and a cashier fall in love. The vast majority of us are simply working our nine to five, trying to make ends meet, saving a nest egg for retirement, and hoping to find some joy at the end of the day.

If we're going to pay money to see a movie, we want the dream, complete with the cherry on top! It's no accident *Pretty Woman* was not about a snaggletooth hooker working a truck stop. Yes, I believe there is someone for everyone, and in most cases there is more than one person who would fit the bill. The important thing for us to keep in mind as we leave the theater is that no one gets everything they want. However, this does not mean you have to settle for less in terms of the most important characteristics and values you require to be happy.

Fear of Dying Alone

Another cause for making an impulsive decision when it comes to choosing a mate is the fear of dying alone. With each passing year or decade, we get subtle reminders that our time here is finite. No woman wants to be the old lady found dead in her home with two cats running around for days before someone discovers her body. And no man wants to think of himself lying on his deathbed in a nursing home without a loved one to hold his hand. One Hollywood example of this need being met comes from the movie *The Notebook*. James Garner's character spends much of the movie retelling his character's wife their love story. The wife, played by Gena Rowlands, is suffering from Alzheimer's disease. There are times when her memory returns for a few minutes and they rejoice in having one another for a brief time. In the end they are found together in bed, passed away.

Or who can forget the following scene in *Titanic*: while the ship is taking on massive amounts of water, we see a mother calming down her kids as they lay in bed, and the camera takes us to an elderly couple spooning in bed as the flood breaks through. "Until death do us part" is mentioned in most wedding vows. The true meaning of having a soul mate is to have someone until the end.

All of the above desires and beliefs are reasons why so many people are willing to continue their pursuit to have someone, anyone, even if only for one night, to hold and be held.

In the end, we choose our own destiny by either following our plans or by being impulsive. Is your current relationship or marriage the result of an impulsive decision? Were there calculated decisions made along the way? Was it coincidence that brought you together?

Were you looking to have a relationship? Did you wake up one day to find yourself in one?

I wrote the following article offering advice to men as to when they should *not* get married. The same advice could easily be applied for women.

5 Reasons Why Men Should Not Get Married

You Don't Know Who You Are

It's almost a cliché to hear someone say they got married too young.

The truth is, marriage and monogamy both require maturity, not only age wise, but also in terms of personal development. Ideally, when you join your life with another person, you should have a handle on who you are, what you want, and what you need in a mate. Keep in mind the answers to these questions are likely to change dramatically, especially from the ages of eighteen to thirty-five. During your early youth, it's very possible all you cared about was having a hot-looking girl with a great sense of humor. As you mature, you realize there are other traits needed as well to have a real shot at marital success.

It takes a reasonable amount of time to formulate your own life philosophy. In addition to doing some major introspective thinking, it's also necessary to have a certain amount of general life experience that should include getting an education or career training, selecting a career path, dating, and traveling. Until you know who you are and have determined what you want, in all likelihood your relationships will come as a result of happenstance or impulsive decisions. Selecting a life partner is one of the most important decisions you will ever make.

You owe it to yourself to make sure your decision comes from a place of awareness.

One of You Is In Significant Debt

There is an old saying that goes, "Romance without finance is nonsense." No matter how prepared someone is, a marriage is bound to have its share of challenges. However, entering into a marriage with a significant debt is a recipe for disaster. You are essentially starting your life together behind the eight ball. Many couples make the mistake of believing things will somehow work out magically. But debt removal is something you have to be diligent about.

Soon after marriage, a lot of couples begin having children. But the joys of parenthood come with a cost. In addition to purchasing food, diapers, and other assorted items, you need to have more money deducted from your payroll check for health insurance purposes. If you are going to have a two-income household, there will likely be daycare expenses.

A mortgage, cars, furnishings, clothing, food, vacations, college funds for the kids, and saving for retirement will be a challenge, but there are also likely to be occasional emergencies and unplanned expenses.

Ideally you want to come into a marriage as debt free as possible.

It's Not Your Idea

If you have to be sold on it, persuaded, or given an ultimatum before proposing, then you are getting married for the wrong reasons. Many men propose simply because it's what their girlfriend wants or expects. Some guys go as far as saying, "She's *earned it* after all we've been together for." Marriage is not some award you bestow upon a woman for time served. It's not something to be decided upon impulsively or by saying, "Why the hell not?" There's a good reason you have not proposed, whether you are aware of it or not. Generally speaking, when a man knows what he wants, he is decisive.

All marriages should at least start off with both people wanting to get married.

She Is Pregnant or Has Given Birth to Your Child

You can be a great father without marrying someone, especially if you don't love the woman. Women ultimately have the right to decide how they will respond to a pregnancy and how much the father is involved. If the only reason you are considering marriage is because there is a child involved, then you are not getting married for the right reasons.

A marriage based upon circumstances rather than love is likely to fail.

You Bore Easily and Constantly Lust after Other Women

One clear signal that you are not ready to "forsake all others" is if you are unable to keep your eyes, thoughts, and fantasies off of other women.

It's a mistake to believe that marriage will make you settle down.

I have known guys who really thought they could fool around with other women all the way up until their wedding day and suddenly change their ways by saying "I do." Wrong! If your motto is "Variety is the spice of life," a monogamous marriage is not for you. There is no sense in wrecking your life trying to be something that is against your nature. Divorces are expensive, and as the common saying goes, "Hell hath no fury like a woman scorned." Trust me; with over seven billion people on the planet, there are enough women out there who will have no problem with no-strings-attached relationships.

A real player lets the women he dates know up front he has no intention of ever getting married. It's just wrong to allow women to get their hopes up for a "happily ever after" ending.

Oddly enough there are lots of women who will be more determined to make you change your tune. However any heartache they experience is clearly on them.

When You Say "I Do"

Marriage is a very serious undertaking. You want to position yourself for the best possible chance for success. Selecting a life partner is one of the most important decisions you will ever make. Dr. James C. Dobson advises, "Don't marry the person you think you can live with; marry only the individual you think you can't live without."

Remember, he who fails to plan, plans to fail.

There are those who realize they have made a mistake in who they've selected as a mate. However, they believe that, given time, they'll be able to change him or her.

We Are Who
We Are

Changing Water into Wine Myth

Albert Einstein said, "Women marry men hoping they will change. Men marry women hoping they will not." Both are being unrealistic!

Men and women have been known to get involved with mates whom they felt lacked some qualities they desired. This would not be a big deal if they also changed their laundry list of requirements for an acceptable mate. However, there are a lot of people that attempt to take someone with potential and mold them into the kind of person they actually want.

Pygmalion and *My Fair Lady* propagate what I call the "changing water into wine" myth. It's based upon the belief that we have the power to take someone who does not have the traits we want and change them into what we want over time.

In *Pygmalion*, a gentleman bets he can pass off a lowly flower girl as a high society lady. I've heard people say their significant other would be perfect if only…

Similar to the fictional story, shortly after making such statements, a project begins to change the partner or spouse.

A woman wishes her man would open doors or pull out her chair.

A man wishes his wife didn't smoke.

Another woman wants her husband to be more romantic.

A husband wishes his wife were more adventurous sexually.

An outgoing person is frustrated with his or her wallflower mate.

The vast majority of the time, we spot these missing traits in a person early on. It's not as though they would be able to hide them from us for eternity. However, we pressed on in the relationship because we saw potential in the other person.

One of the reasons we are willing to take on the challenge of changing a person into what we want is because we have given up on finding someone who already has all the traits we desire. We are determined to turn lemons into lemonade. As mentioned earlier, if we simply accepted people as they are there would be no issue. Alternatively, had we determined the person's behavior or trait to be a deal breaker and moved on, it would not be an issue. It becomes a problem, however, when we attempt to be godlike or act as if we are heroes coming to the rescue. Various methods are employed to initiate change, from subtle suggestions to blatant ultimatums, *once we are assured the person is emotionally invested in our relationship.*

Here are a few examples of how some people begin the change process. They purchase clothes they want their mate to wear, buy colognes and perfumes that appeal to their own sense of smell, recommend their mate try something different with his or her hair, offer unsolicited grammar and diction correction during casual conversations, praise or reward them for behavior they approve of, and pull away physically when the behavior does not fit within their goal.

I once overheard one woman tell her friend, "Girl, you have to train a man!"

Parents, teachers, coaches, mentors, and numerous other role models are responsible for the early development of an individual. Beyond the formative years comes *self-education* and discovery, which leads a person to develop his or her own life philosophy.

Almost every newspaper in America contains an advice column, and on most days you will find at least one letter written along the lines of, "How do I get my spouse to [fill in the blank]?" The real answer is, you don't! The only person you have control over is yourself.

All you can do is ask for what you want. If you are not getting what you want after you've asked and expressed its importance, you have a decision to make. If it's a deal breaker, get out! If it's not, learn to live without! Staying in a relationship where you continue to ask, beg, nag, and complain, hoping one day your mate will give in, leads to frustration on your part and resentment on his or her part. Most of us prefer to be around others who enjoy our company and make us feel good. Therefore, people who feel frustrated, resentful, or unappreciated in relationships are often ripe for an affair.

An Epiphany

One definition for the word epiphany is an illuminating realization or discovery.

The following example comes from my own personal experience of trying to change someone.

Many years ago, I met an attractive woman at a nightclub. We hit it off right away physically and began a casual relationship. I quickly learned Diana had three young daughters. She and her daughters lived with her parents. Diana was receiving government assistance, including food stamps, as well as doing some babysitting for which she was paid under the table. She never watched the news or read the newspaper and had no interest in current events. Beyond passionate chemistry and our love of movies and music, we had very little in common.

Knowing what I know today, I should have realized she was content with her life based upon conversations we had. She never alluded to having any dreams or ambitions beyond keeping me happy physically. Looking back, I suppose it was this trait that kept me coming back. I was in my mid-twenties not looking to get married and just wanted to have a good time. She was a year older than me.

During this time I gradually found myself slipping into more of a Superman role. Diana soon moved out of her parent's home and into a rental town-home a few doors down from them. The place was owned by a woman who was sympathetic to Diana's plight as a single mother. The landlord gave her a great deal on the rent by California standards and promised not to raise it.

To make a long story short, I began to bring groceries over to her house from time to time. I helped the kids with their homework, took Diana shopping, brought the kids to movies and plays, and we all went on a trip to Las Vegas.

Diana did not own a car or have a driver's license. Some weekends I would bring her and the kids to my place, which was located in a much nicer area. I attempted to teach Diana how to utilize checking and savings accounts. She was cashing her welfare check at the liquor store and paying an insane fee to do so. Diana never opened a bank account. I gave her books to read, such as *Think and Grow Rich* and *How to Win Friends and Influence People*, but they were never cracked open.

Our relationship lasted over four years. One day, I had an epiphany of sorts. I realized Diana had no interest in changing her life. In many respects there was no need for her to do so as long as she had me to do the heavy lifting. In another era, I suppose this would have been ideal for a man to have a wife or girlfriend who stayed at home, cleaned the house, looked after the kids, and took care of his every physical need.

I, on the other hand, was longing for an intellectual equal, someone that could occasionally treat me to a dinner out or a weekend getaway, somebody to discuss current events and host dinner parties with, and so forth. In my eyes I had done everything I could to raise Diana's level of awareness, to show her the life she could potentially have by taking certain steps. It hit me one day: "You can't change people who don't want to change."

I'll never forget what she said to me when I ended our relationship: "Thanks for wasting four effing years of my life!" Although I had always been candid with her about my intentions to remain unmarried at that point in life, I was too naïve to realize her take on our relationship was far different from mine.

On reflection, I suppose we were both guilty of attempting to change the other. I thought I could turn her into a strong, financially secure career woman with varied world interests by giving her books and taking her places to inspire her. She thought she could turn me into a husband and father by showering me with love and affection. I was too immature to see that four years out of a single mother's life was dramatically different from four years out of single man's life.

Pinot Noir

On occasion I find myself in the mood for a nice broiled steak with a glass of smooth pinot noir. I have a couple of options open to me.

I could rip up my backyard, plant grape seed, spread fertilizer, and water and nurture the vines for months until the grapes are perfect for picking. Then I'd smash them, add water and sugar, and begin the fermentation process. My next step would be to place the wine in barrels and let it sit for a couple of years until the flavor is divine. I'd then grill or broil my steak and have my glass of pinot noir in two to four years.

My other option is to drive to my local grocery store and pick up a bottle of pinot noir and drink it with my steak dinner tonight. The first option involves *changing* my backyard into a vineyard so I can make a bottle of wine, and the second option is to simply purchase a bottle of wine that *already* exists. There's a big difference between trying to *make* something and buying what you want.

When I was younger, I sought to impose my will in relationships. As I got a little older, I adopted a "sell rather than tell" approach. My rationalization was I'd rather be sold on something than be told to do something. Today I find myself at a point in my life where I simply want to be with someone who naturally wants the same things as me at the same pace that I want them. This ideology requires a real knowledge of self as well as the patience to meet such a person. In the long run it's much better than dealing with the frustration, resentment, and wasted time and energy that comes with trying to change someone.

If you are a woman who wants her man to be romantic, then find a romantic man. If you are a man that wants his lady to be passionate, then find a passionate woman.

Chemistry (I Can Learn to Love Them)

An old man once advised me, "Don't marry someone you love. Marry someone that loves you." In the early 1960s there was a record by Jimmy Soul called *If You Wanna Be Happy* that reached number one on the charts. The song espoused the idea a man would be happy for the rest of his life if he made an ugly girl his wife. The lyrics repeatedly state "Never make a pretty girl your wife." Essentially, both the old man and the song spread the belief that an ugly person will try harder to please you because he or she is more grateful and appreciative to have you.

There's also relationship advice that says the person with the least amount of interest in the relationship controls it. As disparaging as this belief sounds to me, I can understand how it may be true in theory. When a person feels lucky or blessed to have someone special in their life, he or she is inclined to be mindful, appreciative, and more willing to compromise. However, I doubt it's possible to be truly happy with someone you find unattractive and have no chemistry with simply because they are in love with you.

Lori Gottlieb recently wrote a book titled *Marry Him: The Case for Settling for Mr. Good Enough*. But marrying someone because they look good on paper is a far cry from being in love. In order to fall in love with someone, there has to be chemistry. My favorite Bonnie Raitt song is "I Can't Make You Love Me If You Don't." One line in the song states, "You can't make your heart feel something it won't..." It would be nearly impossible to fool someone into believing you are madly in love with him or her for a lifetime. Eventually a number of signs would give you away, such as a lack of affection initiated by you, or if you never give them a lingering glance of appreciation, the kind of look that says, "I can't believe how lucky I am to have you!" People eventually figure it out for themselves, but often they love you so much they are willing to accept what crumbs you toss their way for a certain amount of time.

Sooner or later, an outside force will come along and point out to them they are in love with someone who clearly is not in love with them. It's difficult to avoid the truth when others point it out. Imagine the hurt you'd feel if you realized your spouse was never truly in love with you. They married you for some arbitrary reason. Perhaps they had reached a certain age, you looked good on paper, you were the only one who asked or said yes, they were tired of being single, you were "good enough," you were emotionally safe for them, and probably the worst of all reasons is that *you* were madly in love with them and they knew you'd do anything or give them anything they wanted without requiring much in return.

Each of us deserves to be with someone *we* are in love with and who is in love with us. To do otherwise is to rob yourself and the person you're with of time the two of you could have had with other people that would have been a better fit. Chemistry is not something you want to compromise on when it comes to selecting a life partner.

Chemistry is a double-edged sword. It can lead us to make impulsive decisions as discussed in the previous chapter. It's also a requirement to have any real chance at a long-lasting relationship. Keep in mind chemistry is just one requirement; it is not to be the sole driving force for selecting a mate.

When we ignore chemistry, we run the risk of entering into a relationship with someone who looks good on paper but isn't necessarily the right match for us. This is usually the type of person society indicates is a quality person. The following is an example of such a situation.

John is reliable, dependable, polite, responsible, caring, and possesses a good sense of humor. He is financially and emotionally secure. John takes care of himself physically by eating right and working out, and he maintains a positive attitude toward life. Most of all, he is crazy about Mary. However, Mary is not really attracted to John. There are no sparks, no fireworks, and no hint of excitement when she is around him. It's like putting on an old pair of worn slippers. The relationship is comfortable but lacks exhilaration for her.

Kissing John feels like kissing a wall. Sex with him is unfulfilling and boring. To make matters worse, while Mary contemplates whether she should stay with John, her friends keep telling her how *lucky* she is to have someone like him.

They tease Mary by saying, "If you don't want him, send him over my way." After a while, she begins to downplay the importance of chemistry. Mary accepts a marriage proposal from John with the belief in time she can come to love him and develop that magic spark or convince herself passion is not all that important in having a successful marriage. Wrong! Boredom is one of the leading causes for having an affair.

Passion by Numbers

One school of thought believes it is possible to train or teach someone how to connect with you passionately simply by letting them know how you like to be kissed, touched, held, and so forth. But as was mentioned earlier in this chapter, your mate has to *want* to do things your way or else your instruction will lead to resentment.

The belief here is that chemistry and passion are a matter of mechanics. If this were true, that would mean anyone who did the same exact things to you would make you feel the same exact way. Just because the results may be similar does not make it the same. Masturbation and sexual intercourse can both lead to an orgasm, but most people would prefer intercourse to masturbation. As in life, it's about the journey and not the destination. Such is the case with passion and chemistry.

Yes, you can teach someone how to get the job done. However, that is far from having your world rocked or having an intense desire, attraction, or craving for a specific person. The truth is, you can't create chemistry and you can't manufacture lust and passion. Those who enter into a marriage devoid of natural chemistry will have to decide if they can truly be happy long-term with only the mechanics of passion. This is why it's important to know yourself. Each of us has our own list of requirements we want in a mate, and if chemistry is not high on your list, maybe it's possible for you to make things work with someone you don't experience much . chemistry with.

Another school of thought is to be honest with the person who loves you. Tell him or her you admire all of their great qualities but feel there's a lack of chemistry between you. Your honesty allows this person to make an *informed decision* with regard to pursuing a relationship with you. This approach runs the risk of losing this person who by all accounts looks great on paper. In fact, you may kick yourself should they decide to seek out someone who *naturally* feels passion for them. A part of you may believe you threw a perfectly good fish back into the ocean. However, there is no substitute for honesty when it comes to matters of the heart. Your decision to be upfront about your lack of chemistry is likely the best thing you can do. Each of us deserves to have someone who is madly in love with us.

Your prospective mate may decide they want to stick with you and be willing to learn how to please you. If you decide to proceed with this relationship, it is imperative to show your appreciation for his or her efforts and be willing to reciprocate by initiating affection. There has to be mutual give and take; otherwise you may run the risk of having your mate come to resent you. Whenever there is a perception of one person having to jump through hoops to please another without reciprocation, it can cause them to think you are not worth it. Therefore it's important to be interested in finding out what turns him or her on. When you are with a loving person, you each get back as much as you give.

If you find you don't care what pleases your significant other, odds are you not only lack chemistry with this person but you also do not love them. Eventually he or she will either seek to be adored by someone else or bump into another person who does shower them with attention. No one wants to be a servant forever. Love, affection, and effort are a two-way street.

All or Nothing

The final school of thought is all or nothing. These people refuse to settle for anything less than the complete package. This option requires patience and discipline. Knowing what you want is very important, but it's also important to know the value of what you bring to the table. There are far too many people who want the moon but have nothing to offer in return. *Don't expect to sit next to the moon unless you are a star*! It's imperative to keep growing, learning, and evolving as a person. As time goes on, more than likely your list of needs or requirements in a mate will change.

This approach to life does not mean one has to live like a nun or a monk. It merely means you will consciously decide how far a relationship goes and who you will spend time with. There is no particular deadline for finding the person that is right for you. The odds are in your favor! With over seven billion people on the planet, there is more than one person who will fulfill your requirements.

Look back on your current or most recent relationship and try to recall how you met, where you met, and how you felt when you met. Did your heart melt upon first sight? Was it a mere ember that grew brighter over time? Keep in mind there is nothing objectively wrong or right with that person. They're simply right or wrong for *you*. The very traits you have come to despise in your significant other, another person may find endearing. There is someone who will love and appreciate each of us just as we are. It's unrealistic to expect liars to be honest, thieves to be trustworthy, and cheaters to be loyal. Life is too short to spend your time trying to change water into wine or teaching cats how to bark!

Difference of Opinions

You might disagree with what I have said in this chapter.. It's possible you have decided to continue with your project of changing water into wine. There is a whole industry dedicated to teaching you how to change your mate.

There are therapists that specialize in offering techniques for the sake of changing your spouse. There are also loads of books out there that promote the notion you have the power to make someone over into what you want them to be. One such book is *How to Change Your Spouse and Save Your Marriage* by Joel Kotin. The author shares his nine techniques for creating change in your spouse:

Six weeks without criticism

Increase communication

Negotiation

Mediation

Behavioral conditioning

Manipulation

Personal growth

The ultimatum

Professional help

One problem I have with such books is their assumption the reader is perfect, and it's his or her significant other that needs to be fixed. Chapters consisting of manipulation, behavioral conditioning, and giving ultimatums personally give me reason to pause. Nonetheless, my intention is not to knock books of this nature but rather to remind you that there are those who disagree with me. You always have the option to invest time in making attempts to mold your mate into something that better suits you.

There are many of you who have been in relationships or marriages for quite a while. You may have children together, or your finances may be so intertwined it would be a nightmare for you to throw in the towel and walk away. In cases such as these, it might make sense for you to give books such as the one previously described a shot.

It takes courage to look at the truth of a situation and make a change.

It takes patience and tolerance to accept people as they are.

Most importantly, you must know yourself well enough to determine what you can and cannot live with. None of us are perfect, but no one should have to accept living with someone who has too many deal-breaker qualities. I personally subscribe to the belief that change comes from within. A person has to want to change. The only person you have real control over is yourself. For those of you who are in bad relationships, the only thing I could imagine being worse would be staying in the same situation for another day, another month, or another year. It may be time for you to make some changes.

There are basically two types of people: those that spend their time shopping for a bottle of wine of their choice, and those who are determined to spend their time changing water into wine. Miracles have been known to happen, but counting on one to happen in your case might not be the best approach to solving problems in a relationship.

Don't **Assume** Communication **Will** Lead to **Action**

The Communication Myth

It seems that whenever a couple is having problems, the old cliché "communication is the key" is quickly offered as the solution. Common sense also dictates that if you want something, you should ask for it. One factor that is almost never mentioned in these cases is that in order for communication to have a shot at changing things, both people have to still give a damn about the relationship. If one or both people only care about what *they* will get out of a situation, then having one person talking and another nodding in agreement is equivalent to talking to a wall.

"Going along to get along" is not communication. It's trying to get someone to shut up. Real communication involves both parties contributing to a discussion, providing suggestions, and offering their insight as to how things got where they are. Both parties should be engaged in the conversation. Having someone quickly say, "Okay, okay, all right…" just to shut you up is the same as having them say "whatever" or "Here we go again." There is no understanding or empathetic listening taking place.

It's a myth to believe all one needs to do is ask for something and it will be automatically given. One has to explore why you have not been getting what you want. Rarely do you hear of couples having a communication problem in the *beginning* of a relationship. In my opinion, there are two main reasons for this.

> When we are in the infatuation phase of a relationship, we don't want to say anything that may push away the person we want to win over, or we're simply blind when it comes to his or her flaws.

> In the beginning, he or she was doing everything we dreamed of without us needing to ask. Making sure we were happy was paramount on his or her list of things to do.

I will go into further detail regarding relationship beginnings in the chapter *Unrealistic Romantic Myths*. The following comes from an article I wrote in 2010.

Communication: Why Do We Hate Asking in Relationships?

John and Amy have been married for five years. When John comes home from work, he says hello to Amy while sifting through the mail. Afterward he goes upstairs to change his clothes and heads out to the gym.

Early on in their relationship, John would come home and the first thing he would do was hug and kiss Amy. They used to spend time with each other after work talking about their day, laughing about things, cooking dinner together, and cleaning up the kitchen together. One night, Amy follows John upstairs to communicate with him about this. She tells him she misses him greeting her with a kiss and a hug. The very next day when John arrives home, he gives Amy a short hug and a quick dry kiss and heads toward the mail.

Amy is not happy. She wants to go back to the romantic times they had in the beginning.

Why Do We Hate Asking in Relationships?

A part of us is upset because we feel we shouldn't have to ask for things that were once given to us freely. Even if your partner gives you exactly what you *asked* for, oftentimes there is still a sour taste of resentment in your mouth.

There is a scene in the movie *The Break-Up* where Jennifer Aniston argues with Vince Vaughn over household chores. She says, "I want you *to want to* do the dishes!" When you get *your way*, you know you're being appeased by your spouse or significant other not because it was something *they desired to do* but simply because you asked them to do it. Essentially, Vince's crime was not being thoughtful or considerate to her wants and needs. Jennifer felt taken for granted and believed her man should have offered her help.

In many ways, it's a no-win situation. If you ask for something and get it, you're unhappy because it wasn't the other person's idea. If you ask for something and you don't get it, that's another issue.

Cold Hard Facts

There are two basic reasons why your mate would not give you something you have asked for multiple times.

1. They don't have it to give.

2. They don't feel you're worth the effort to give it to.

If you're not getting what you want, you have a major decision to make.

1. If it's a deal breaker, get out.

2. If it's not a deal breaker, learn to live without.

Beating your head against the wall while trying to change water into wine will only lead to frustration for you and resentment for the person you're in a relationship with. People change when *they* want to change.

"Communication" Has a Negative Connotation

Whenever someone says, "We need to talk" or "We have a communication problem," we anticipate the conversation will contain some type of complaint, something negative, or an uncomfortable subject matter. Ironically, we're communicating all day long at work in meetings, on the phone, and via e-mail. Therefore we know the act of communicating is not inherently a bad thing at all. The difference in those situations is that we do not feel the need to announce that we have something to say. It's the formality of scheduling a time to discuss something that turns most people off or puts them in a defensive mode.

The only thing worse for some people than having to ask for something is being asked. No one enjoys hearing the gravity that comes with the words "Can we talk?" An ominous feeling materializes in the air. The next time you have something to discuss with your spouse or significant other, simply wait for the appropriate time, be considerate, and say what's on your mind! There's no need to set up an agenda complete with a PowerPoint presentation.

Therapy Has Its Limits!

There are times when a couple determines they need a mediator when discussing issues in their relationship. Going to see a therapist is often nothing more than going through the motions of checking off a box on the road to divorce. One or both parties have decided in their mind the marriage is over, but by going to therapy they can at least tell the world they gave it a shot. It's the equivalent of trying to put out a house fire with a water pistol. Waiting too long to address problems in therapy is a waste of your money and time. I speak from personal experience.

My first wife and I were having problems in our marriage. Initially it began with financial troubles. We purchased a brand new town-home in Southern California at the height of the real estate boom during the early 1990s. The price with upgrades was close to two hundred thousand dollars. We closed escrow with 10 percent down on Friday, December 13, 1991.Like most couples buying their first home, we exhausted everything we had in savings to make the purchase. Naturally, a new home means new furniture, so we put our credit cards to use. We had the place set up at showroom level in about two weeks and hosted a New Year's Eve party. By the end of April 1992, we had both been laid off from our respective aerospace company jobs. In less than four months after purchasing our town-home, we were trying to pay the mortgage, homeowner's association fees, utilities, and various debts with unemployment checks and checks issued as lines of credit from a couple of our credit cards. Romance and passion went out the window and stressful times ruled the day. Financial and emotional bankruptcy soon followed.

Quiet Before the Storm

When the smoke cleared, we were able to keep our town-home and our two cars that were paid for. We both got new jobs but we were never the same. We began to socialize apart from one another with friends each of us had before we met.

One day we had a heated exchange after I noticed she had been charging up new debt with credit cards she recently received from a few department stores. Among the purchases were a new patio set, an Australian leather coat, and a collection of decorative plates. Up until this point in our marriage, we had joint accounts and she paid all the bills. I went through some of the statements and saw she had us almost up to five thousand dollars in debt and was only making minimum payments. When my wife came home, I suggested we go back to having separate bank accounts and split the common household bills in half. Each of us would then buy what we wanted for ourselves out of the money we had left over in our respective accounts.

The closest thing I can use to describe what happened next would be a scene out of *The Exorcist*. Her head appeared to spin around as she slowly said the following (one inch from my face) in a demonic voice with each word being louder than the previous, "I'm not going to live that way!" I managed to regroup, and I grabbed her arms while looking into her eyes. I asked the following question, "Do you want me to kill you?"

A deafening silence engulfed the room. I quickly ran upstairs and moved everything I owned out of the master bedroom into the guest bedroom. A couple of days later, a telephone technician rang the doorbell and informed me she was there to install a new phone line in the guest room. The message was clear. I was not to answer the primary house phone.

Weeks went by with us attending company functions together, returning home, and going to our separate rooms. One day she suggested we go see a therapist.

Let the Sessions Begin

Our first therapist was of the low-rent variety, and our sessions were around twenty-five dollars each.

My wife led the discussion with talk of "power struggles" between us and my not helping her with the household chores. I sat there patiently waiting for my turn to speak. When it was my turn, I explained to the therapist that after witnessing my wife remake the bed after I made it, refold the towels after I folded them, and being told the only way to clean a toilet was by sticking my hand into the bowl with a cloth and swishing it around with cleaning products, I had decided to let her do things *her way*.

At one point I suggested we divide the home up with each of assigned to clean an area. She could take upstairs and I would take downstairs, or vice versa. This way she would not feel as though she had to tackle the whole house, and I could clean up my section my way. Her response to my suggestion was, "No, I don't want to do it that way." That's when I knew my wife had no interest in making compromises. The therapist sat there dumbfounded. He began by making some suggestions to her regarding letting go of her need to control some things. That was the last time we saw that guy.

My wife told me she wanted to continue therapy to save our marriage, but she felt the low-rent guy we had been seeing was going to be moving too slowly to resolve our issues. During the early nineties, there was a very popular psychiatrist based in the Los Angeles area named Dr. David Viscott. He was on the radio, he had a syndicated television show, and he had written books. One of his books was titled *I Love You, Let's Work It Out*. He conducted workshops and seminars and created The Viscott Center for Natural Therapy. There were locations in Beverly Hills, Newport Beach, and Pasadena, California. We lived in Orange County and opted to go to the Newport Beach office.

The building was brand new, and the offices were immaculate. A session with Dr. Viscott himself cost approximately $1200 an hour. We decided to go with one of his staff therapists, which cost us three hundred dollars per hour. If you've ever been to a therapist, you know the scheduled "hour" is actually forty-five minutes long.

The doctor explained to us that he would be recording our sessions and giving us each a taped copy along with some workbook exercises to take home. The following session, we would review what had taken place and move forward from there. Once again, my wife was given the opportunity to speak first. She began the session by saying, "A few weeks ago, he threatened to kill me." I could not believe she said that!

I sat there stunned, watching the tape recorder document every word she was saying. When my turn came to speak, I mumbled something about having power struggles. We never went back for another session, and neither one of us cracked open a workbook.

A few weeks later, she went to Arizona to visit one of her single girlfriends for the weekend. One of my friends came by the house on Sunday and I ended up grilling a couple of steaks and making some macaroni. After dinner, he left and I washed the dishes.

The following morning I came downstairs and there was a note left for me on the kitchen counter with a kernel of macaroni on it. The note read, "Please leave things the way you found them."

I ran upstairs to my room to get some paper along with Dale Carnegie's book *How to Win Friends and Influence People*. I wrote a note saying, "You really need to read this book!" The following day I saw she had set the book afire on the stove! Quickly I gathered the remains of the book along with the ashes and placed them in a bag, which I hid in the trunk of my car.

My thinking at the time was that if our therapist tape with the so-called death threat came up during divorce proceedings, I'd submit the destroyed book as evidence of her violent nature. Thankfully we had an amicable divorce in the end.

Motivations and Objectives

One of the many reasons communication and therapy often do not work is because each person in the relationship may have a different agenda. When I look back, my wife and I did not enter therapy because we wanted to renew our love, learn to compromise, or build a stronger relationship. She wanted a "professional" to take her side, hoping it would influence me enough to go along with her program. I, on the other hand, had come to the conclusion that we were not right for each other. Having a parent/child relationship would never work for me. But I agreed to give therapy a chance because I did not want to look bad to friends and family.

The day you start thinking about your relationship in terms of "you and me" instead of "us and we" is the day your relationship begins to die. When your spouse's happiness is no longer important to you, it's time to move on. Simply put, when you're in love with someone, you want him or her to be happy. If someone is in love with you, they want you to be happy. A couple that is in love and wants the best for each other will likely benefit the most from therapy and communication sessions. They are more likely to approach their problems looking for a way to compromise, which will help their relationship evolve. When the people in a relationship have different ideologies, one or both are most likely looking for a way to gain individual victories in every situation, which eventually leads to the dissolution of the relationship.

My marriage did not fail because of our financial troubles. Many couples in love face financial hard times together. They create a plan together, roll up their sleeves, and rebuild. Our financial problems served as a magnifying glass to examine other underlying issues. It was just easier to ignore our problems when we were afloat. A problem is nothing more than an opportunity for us to take a time out and reassess the decisions we have made and to develop a better strategy moving forward.

I don't believe in engaging in a game of "sinners and saints" when it comes to discussing exes. After all, every friend, lover, or spouse in your life is someone you said yes to at some point. I can't escape the fact that it was I who proposed to my ex-wife. She, on the other hand, bears responsibility for saying yes to my proposal. It's not a case of her being right or me being wrong. We were just wrong for each other, and even attempting to work on our habits of communication was not a solution.

A Happy
Relationship Is the
Result of a
Labor of Love

Relationship Work Myth

"It takes a lot of work to make a relationship work" has been stated so often that most of us buy into a scenario where we expect love to be the equivalent of taking a roller coaster ride filled with numerous ups and downs. We expect major obstacles, personality clashes, and drama-filled nights. Accepting these beliefs as gospel has led to more couples enduring relationships they had no business being in. There is an assumption that every couple deals with the same issues.

The number one cause for divorce is and has always been selecting the wrong mate! There is no amount of communication or work that can overcome being with someone who does not want what you want. One of the reasons people end up selecting the wrong mate is because they don't know themselves as well as they should. They don't know what they want in a mate. Too many people go with their impulses when it comes to selecting a mate.

A lot of thinking and consideration should take place before exchanging vows with anyone. It takes more time to get to know someone than most people are willing to invest.

Some people put more research into selecting a car than selecting a spouse. Even when you do have a handle on who you are and what you want out of life, remember that you will change over time. What works for you today may not be what you want in ten or twenty years. This is why it's important to communicate during a marriage to make sure you are growing in the same direction and not growing apart. Society would probably be better off if more people waited until they were thirty or thirty-five before getting married and starting a family.

Following the marital advice of your parents and grandparents may not serve you well. Marriage expectations of couples today are completely different from expectations of couples from a few generations ago. The household model of the *Leave it to Beaver* era, where the wife stayed home, baked cookies, cleaned the house, and ran the household budget, is long gone.

Historically, marriage meant men would provide for the family's financial needs and women would take care of the household needs. Sex would take place on a regular basis and most meals would be home cooked. In the event there was a divorce, the husband would move out of the house. He would become a weekend parent while continuing to support his ex-wife and children financially.

Once the sexual revolution was in full swing and women joined the workforce in record numbers, the dynamics of married life changed. Better birth control options for women allowed for an increase in premarital sex and reduced the odds of accidental pregnancies. Society has also become more accepting of non-married couples living together. Marriage is now an unnecessary legal hurdle in the eyes of many people. As women have become more equal to men in the work force, they are less inclined to get married at younger ages. It is not unheard of for a successful single woman to opt for motherhood through adoption or artificial insemination with no plans to get married.

Today most couples are made up of two independent and employed people. It is not uncommon for both people to have 401(k)s or pension plans in place by the time they get married. In many instances when a couple gets married after finishing college and building a career, there is a good chance both parties already own their own homes. Prenuptial, postnuptial, and trust agreements are almost a routine aspect for many successful people entering into marriage.

In a time where both sexes experience a measure of financial independence, many social stigmas have been removed. Couples are opting to live together, have children born out of wedlock, or remain single for life. One wonders why anyone would choose to enter into a marriage, which requires a lot of hard work to maintain. It's not exactly a selling point. The word single conjures up freedom for some people and loneliness for others. Marriage and committed relationships are thought to be restrictive by some, but others love the thought of being attached to someone they can count on through ups and downs. Perception is reality.

Work versus a Labor of Love

Work is usually defined as a sustained physical or mental effort to overcome obstacles and achieve an objective. It's doing one thing when you would rather be doing something else. A large majority of the work most couples find themselves dealing with actually involves making an effort to change water into wine or learning to navigate through a communication maze as was discussed in previous chapters.

The motivational speaker Jim Rohn once said, "Work harder on yourself than you do on your job." There is a lot of work one should do on him- or herself prior to making or accepting a marriage proposal.

Any personal to-do list should contain some introspective thinking and writing down exactly what you want out of life. Once you know what you want out of life, the next step is to make a plan. It goes without saying you want to spend time with people who are on the same path or those who offer you encouragement as you pursue your goals.

In the workbook section of this book I will offer some suggestions in selecting a mate. The main focus for now is on you and your wants. Knowing what you want makes it much easier to avoid people and things that keep you from living the life you have chosen for yourself. Remember, every friend, lover, or spouse you have had in your life is due to your saying yes when the opportunity arose to spend time together.

It's important for you to learn to read people similar to the way a FBI profiler does. This means not only do you hear what a person says, but you also note the things they do not say. It's also important to observe how they handle stressful situations and disappointments, especially those you may have something to do with.

Opposites Attract but Only in the Short-term

It's natural to be somewhat fascinated by someone who is your complete opposite. However, you can imagine how much work would be required in spending your life with someone who wants to go left when you want to go right. Over time, those opposite traits that attracted you will be the same ones that frustrate you. Generally speaking, water seeks its own level and like attracts like. People who are compatible have fewer disagreements and less work to do on their relationship.

Relationships evolve over time, and sometimes what we wanted at one stage of our life no longer suits us. Communicating your desire for a change of direction might be necessary. Your mate may be open to trying to do things differently. It's also possible he or she may feel as though you pulled a bait and switch on them. One of the main attractions to having a long-term relationship is stability. Sometimes a drastic change in behavior by one individual can lead to conflict within the relationship. We will revisit this in the "Seasons Change" chapter.

A labor of love can be defined as an undertaking that provides *pleasure* within the work itself as you strive to reach a goal. This is the type of approach that's required to maintain a happy relationship. The following are a few examples of a labor of love.

A childless couple is finally able to conceive and is blessed to have a baby boy. Raising an infant requires early morning feedings, diaper changing, and figuring out what the baby is trying to express when crying.

A young couple purchases their first home, which is a fixer-upper. They spend most weekends going back and forth to Home Depot to purchase items for repairs.

A child persuades her parents to let her have a dog. She now has the task of feeding him, walking him, bathing him, and removing his waste.

A woman decides to plant a vegetable garden in her backyard. She spends several hours getting the dirt ready, selecting the type of seeds to plant, watering the space, pulling weeds, and installing a small fence to discourage pests from entering.

In each of the above scenarios, the "work" described is actually a labor of love. There is a difference between having to work to pay your bills and making a choice to enter into a relationship that requires your time and effort to nurture it.

No one has to enter into a relationship or a marriage, have children, buy a home, plant a garden, or own a pet. However, if you have decided to do so, then the responsible and mature thing is to nurture what you have instead of neglecting it. Relationship work is not about doing something you'd rather not do. It's about looking for the best way to sustain your loving partnership. The hard work is in determining what you want in a partner and selecting the right mate. Once you have accomplished this, you can put most of your focus on keeping the romance alive!

We Choose Our Own Reality

Unrealistic Romantic Myth

It was a day from hell.

Angela had been in meetings all day, and her presentation wasn't due until the end of the day. C-level executives were in town for a quarterly business review meeting. They were grilling each presenter with rapid-fire questions regarding each slide. As Angela sat in the conference room, terrified, she thought back to her honeymoon in Bora Bora. It was just six short months ago but now seemed like a lifetime past.

She remembered Michael and herself making love on the glass-bottomed floor of their over-water bungalow while exotic fish swam beneath them. She thought back to the warm nightly breezes and burning tiki torches as they sat outdoors wining and dining for hours without a care in the world. The honeymoon had been the best vacation of her life.

A loud clap of thunder and a streak of lightning brought Angela's focus back to the meeting. The rain poured down as if in cadence with a Riverdance performance. Angela glanced down at her agenda sheet and saw the lunch break was coming after the current presentation was finished.

Angela felt as though she were dying slowly with each agonizing PowerPoint presentation. She wished her team had been chosen to go first, which would have allowed her to relax the rest of the day. During lunch, her stomach tightened from nerves as she played with her salad and attempted to engage in a conversation with her co-worker Debbie.

After lunch, another three hours crawled by until it was Angela's turn to speak. Nerves took over her body to a point where she almost did not recognize her own voice as she spoke. Her words sounded as if they were coming from a lamb. With each new slide she presented, Angela was questioned concerning the various matrix of raw leads versus net leads and the percentage of those that became sales. By the time Angela had gone over all of the marketing campaigns for the quarter, she was ready to collapse.

At 5:00 p.m. Angela breathed a sigh of relief as she gathered up her laptop, put on her coat, and grabbed her umbrella. Upon stepping outdoors, a gust of wind blew her umbrella inside out and the rain pounded on her as she ran toward her car. Once she started the car and got onto the street, she was met with bumper-to-bumper traffic. At this point Angela burst into tears. Her normal forty-minute commute home was extended to two hours.

Angela walked into the house and detected the scent of garlic in the air along with the relaxing sounds of Andrea Bocelli. Michael stood over a boiling pot of pasta and stirred tomato sauce in another pot. He looked at Angela standing in the kitchen, soaking wet, and he pointed his finger in the direction of the stairs.

Angela walked towards the stairs where she saw a trail of red rose petals ascending up the staircase. She followed the petals all the way into the master bathroom where her eyes fell upon a tub filled with bubbles and surrounded by lit scented candles.

After relaxing and soaking in the tub for an hour, Angela exited the bathroom to find rose petals leading toward their king size bed. Along the side of the bed, Michael had set up a table consisting of pasta, vodka sauce, garlic bread, a bottle of wine, and a couple of pieces of chocolate. They ate dinner in bed and afterward Michael gave her a full body massage. He tenderly made love to her as she climaxed with silent screams. Tears of joy slowly rolled down her cheeks.

The following day she shared the details of her evening with her co-worker Debbie. "You know what kind of day I had yesterday, right? Well let me tell you what Michael did when I got home…" As she spilled events of the evening, she found herself fanning away tears to avoid messing up her makeup. She ended the conversation by saying; "I'm going to love this man until the day I die!"

Five Years Later

It's another day from hell.

Once again, the C-level executives are in town for quarterly meetings. The stress level is high, and to make matters worse, it is raining cats and dogs. Just as before, Angela finds herself in bumper-to-bumper traffic on the way home, which stretches her commute to two hours. When Angela arrives home, Michael is cooking away, music is playing, scented candles are lit, and there are rose petals leading up the stairway. Angela takes in the scene, and without speaking to Michael, she heads upstairs and slams the bedroom door.

The next day she tells her co-worker Debbie the following: "You know what kind of day I had yesterday, right? I got drenched walking to my car because my umbrella blew inside out. It took me over two hours to get home in bumper-to-bumper traffic, and when I finally dragged my ass into the house, my a-hole of husband expected to have sex!"

Debbie replies, "That's a man for you. They only think about themselves."

Cynics versus Romantics

The first six to twelve months of a new relationship is filled with passionate sex, romantic gestures, dates, travel, fun, and laughter. It's at this point one or both people begin to explore the idea of going to "the next level." This ranges from moving in together to getting engaged. They expect it would mean the end of packing overnight bags, driving back and forth across town, and saying sad good-byes as the weekend concludes. Best of all, you will be in each other's arms every night making love until sunup.

But this is not reality. One of the little truths that married couples and couples who live together seldom share with their single friends is that romance, passion, and sex dwindle the more time you spend together. In fact, the same people are likely to have more sex with each other over a long weekend while living *apart* than they would in the course of a week living together! When one person is a guest and the other is a host, it's like having vacation sex. There are no mundane discussions; you want to make the most of your time together. Every weekend is a romantic weekend.

Cynics or "practical" people will tell you having less romance and passionate sex in a long-term relationship is normal. Life gets in the way and other things have a higher priority. However, I have never heard of a couple waking up one day and saying, "Let's have less sex, stop flirting with each other, stop taking showers together, stop leaving naughty voice mails, stop writing love notes to each other, and drop oral sex." Neither do they say, "No more long wet kisses, massages, lighting candles, playing music, setting a romantic mood, or sex outside of the bedroom."

Romantics or "unrealistic" people believe their relationship will only get more passionate, loving, and romantic as time goes on. In fact, they believe that love grows deeper as the years go by. The better you know someone, the more trust there is between you. You become more comfortable with trying new and exciting things with your mate. A romantic is usually sentimental. They recall first kisses, first dates, who wore what, conversations, promises made, and they genuinely believe their lives will be just as they discussed countless times. In an ideal world, if two romantics found each other, their relationship would be heavenly. Two cynics would live in perfect harmony getting exactly what they expected.

The main reason the right pairings seldom get together is because *cynics behave like romantics in the beginning of a new relationship*. This leads to heartache and disappointment for a romantic when the cynic reverts back to his or her natural self.

By the time a cynic reveals his or her true nature, the romantic is emotionally invested in the relationship. He or she tries to keep the fire burning until one day realizing the romantic energy he or she is expending is not being reciprocated, or worse, the other person repeatedly shoots down romantic suggestions.

After having the wind taken out of his or her sail and getting rejected repeatedly, the romantic strives to adapt to the cynic's world by "going along to get along." Eventually the relationship settles into what the cynic calls normal. If the romantic works up the courage to complain about how badly things have changed, he or she is told they are being unrealistic. Cynics usually get their way. It takes less energy for a romantic to stop making romantic gestures than for a cynic to put forth the effort to keep passion alive.

Greeting Card Clues

Something as simple as picking up a greeting card for the holidays can become a challenge. When couples first begin dating or fall in love, there appear to be a million great Hallmark cards you could give your mate that *honestly express* how you're feeling. However, years later, it seems to take more time to find the appropriate card.

A few years back, a male friend of mine went to several stores before finding the right Valentine's card. He wasn't overjoyed with his marriage at the time. Ironically, his wife gave him the same exact card! He went on to tell me, "I know what I was thinking when I bought the card for her, and now I know she must have been thinking and feeling the same way." The card exchange served as a wake-up call for their relationship.

Naturally there are those of us who just grab any card to give their significant other regardless of whether the prose accurately describes our feelings. I imagine these are the same type of people who subscribe to the "tell them what they want to hear" philosophy. The following questions are for those people who believe greeting cards should express their genuine feelings.

If you're having a difficult time finding the right greeting card, does this mean there are underlying issues in your relationship?

If you gave your mate a card which read "For the Love of My Life" and in return you got a card that read "For Someone Special," would you be hurt or disappointed?

Would you read anything into a pattern of your mate giving you only humorous cards while you were giving them cards containing romantic, heartfelt prose?

Would it bother you if your lover or spouse didn't give you a Valentine's, birthday, or Christmas card?

Going beyond greeting card exchanges, what is most important is how you treat each other on a daily basis. Cynics are inclined to believe if a romantic has stopped pushing for more weekend getaways, date nights, and cuddle time, this means they are now on the same page. When it comes to relationships, silence does not necessarily imply agreement. The following comes from an article I wrote regarding beginnings.

Relationships: Do We Save Our Best for the Beginning?

It seems early on in life we're taught to behave differently with new people, new things, and new opportunities. Clichés such as "Dress to impress," "You never get a second chance to make a first impression," and "Always put your best foot forward" are offered up as wise advice. Most people appreciate the new and take the old for granted in many different situations.

We put more effort into getting something than we do to keep it.

The Novelty Effect

A man interviewing for a new position expresses enthusiasm. He is full of positive energy and is genuinely grateful for the new opportunity. He shows up to work fifteen minutes early Monday morning to begin his day to show his dedication. Five years later, he's twenty minutes late. When a co-worker makes a comment about it, he responds, "They're lucky I showed up!"

Someone buys a new car. They wash and wax it every weekend. They have it detailed every six months. Two years later, it's got an inch of dirt on it and the interior looks like a grenade went off.

A couple just started dating. The man comes by the woman's house one Saturday afternoon. She offers to make him a sandwich or cook him something to eat. Five years later, this same man asks, "Honey, will you make me a sandwich?"

She says, "You've got two hands. Fix it yourself!"

Change Brings Change

One day you look up and that special someone walks out of your life, or the exciting career opportunity you had briefly is now being eliminated.

Some things are beyond our control, and no matter how much effort we exert, a happy ending was not in the cards. However, if we're being honest, in most instances we let things slide and we stop putting in the same kind of effort we did in the beginning.

In essence, when we changed, our circumstances changed.

Sofas and Gardens

Relationships are more like gardens than sofas. When you get a new sofa, you bring it home, pick out a spot for it, and pretty much leave it alone. A lot of people take the same approach with relationships and marriages. They think, "Now that I'm married I can relax or "I'm so glad to be out of the dating scene." They stop working out, they pack on the pounds, stop flirting with their mates, stop seducing one another, stop taking showers together, stop buying flowers or sending cards for no reason, stop complimenting each other, stop gazing into each other's eyes, stop listening intently, stop being open to new things and suggestions, stop having candlelight dinners, and stop trying to surprise each other. They lull themselves into believing there is no competition out there. In other words, they stop being the people that won the hearts of their mate! How many times have you heard someone say, "He [or she] is not the same person I fell in love with"?

After the relationship ends, this person finds himself back in the dating scene. The cycle repeats itself. Suddenly they're working out, losing weight, dressing nice, trying new things, and in some instances these are things they refused to do with their ex! They'll say yes to anything rather than risk losing the opportunity to be with a new person they are attracted to in the beginning.

There are many who say becoming lazy is natural. However, no one says to someone they just met, "I hope you know in a year, five years, or ten years from now,

I won't be doing all these nice things for you! You can forget about wild passionate sex. I hate going to musicals. Oral sex will be a thing of the past. The only reason I went to the game, the ballet, or shopping with you was because I thought you were hot! Once you are mine, I won't feel the need to impress your ass!"

It's been said relationships and marriages require work. But most of that work should take place in the selection process. Knowing who you are and what you want is important as you determine whether or not a person shares your goals and agrees with your approach to achieving relationship happiness. The screening process is where the real work lies. The rest of the work is about making sure you are staying on track. Much like the work required in a garden—pulling weeds, planting new seeds, watering, nurturing, and fighting to keep the pests out— it's an ongoing labor of love.

Always keep in mind that whatever you are taking for granted, someone else would be glad to have. Competition for something worthwhile never dies. Whether it is a prime position at a company or a wonderful companion, someone wants what you have. Never stop working to keep what you've earned, and let those around you know your best is yet to come. May your relationship be like a fine wine getting better with time. Any champion will tell you that winning the title is easier than holding onto it. The challenger is usually hungrier than the titleholder.

We would all do well to remember the lyrics from an Impressions song, "The same thing it took to get your baby is the same thing it's going to take to keep them."

Keep in mind you can only change yourself. People change when and if they want to.

The preceding article was written under the assumption the cynic wants to change for love. If you are a cynic, there is still hope for you.

A Secret Lover's Calendar

Some people are blessed with a natural ability to set their mind on a goal and take the necessary actions to make it happen. There are others who have no problem being dedicated to the fulfillment of a goal that is important to them. However, if the goal is not near the top of their priority list, it's difficult for them to stay motivated. One example is someone who desires to lose twenty pounds. They realize they must burn more calories than they take in, exercise, cut back on carbohydrates, drink plenty of water, avoid high fat processed meats, and weigh themselves once a week to track their progress.

Knowing what to do does not automatically translate into doing it. A person may hate going to the gym, but after the workout they're glad they went. This is often true of the cynic who desires to be more romantic. Sometimes the cynic loses track of time and does not realize how long it has been since he or she has done something special to show appreciation for his or her significant other. Creating a habit that does not come naturally requires some help. If you are the cynic in the relationship, one of the best things you can do is to create a secret "lover's calendar" for yourself. You may want to keep it at work or some other place where your mate is not likely to find it.

Take a calendar and circle all the special event dates that apply to your relationship, such as his or her birthday, your various anniversaries (e.g., the day you met, your first date, and your day of engagement), noteworthy Hallmark days like Valentine's Day, Christmas, and New Year's Eve, and long weekends such as Memorial Day, Labor Day, and Thanksgiving. These are all ideal dates for doing something special for your significant other.

During the uneventful months, you also want to target at least one day to surprise him or her. Your goal is to have something to look forward to each month. This may range from you cooking a special meal, performing a chore normally done by your significant other, going to a movie, going to a play or a concert, taking an evening walk in a park or along a beach, having a picnic, or taking a weekend getaway or vacation. It may also include leaving a love note on the bathroom mirror or a loving voice mail at work, bringing home flowers, sending an e-mail greeting card, giving a sensual massage, or planning a surprise seduction.

The calendar is for your eyes only. It's not necessary to have all of your events listed ahead of time. You may want to place a star or mark on one day each month to do something. Once the activity or event is over, make a notation of what you did. Although you will be doing something each month, you want to avoid doing the same things too soon or annually on the same day. The goal is to be unpredictable and have fun with it.

Utilizing this calendar ensures you are doing something to keep the romance alive in your relationship, and if you're fortunate enough to be involved with a romantic, then you will spend the rest of your lives passionately *one-upping* each other.

It's not unrealistic to expect to have a romantic and passionate relationship. It just requires making it a priority in your life. We choose our reality. If the cynics were right about it being natural for passion to die in long-term relationships, it would be generally accepted, and there would be no market for books and workshops dedicated to rekindling the romantic spark in relationships. It's apparent most people don't want to have bland, passionless relationships. They spend millions of dollars each year in an attempt to recapture what has been lost.

It's easier to maintain a fire than it is to reignite a spark!

Monogamy Is a Lifestyle Choice Not a Genetic Code

Monogamy Myth

Marriage requires a special talent, like acting. Monogamy requires genius.

—Warren Beatty

Promiscuity is like never reading past the first page. Monogamy is like reading the same book over and over.

—Mason Cooley

Men would like monogamy better if it sounded less like monotony.

—Rita Rudner

As illustrated by the above quotations, it seems everyone has an opinion about monogamy. Many of us strive to achieve it much like going on a strict diet after eating everything in sight. Others are like addicts giving up their drug of choice in order to lead a healthier lifestyle. Their view of monogamy is that they are making a sacrifice or giving up something they love. They get by one hour, one day, one week, one month, and one year at a time.

Another group of people believes monogamy comes naturally when a couple realizes they are soul mates. Simply put, now that you have found "the one," you become blind to everyone else. Temptation does not stand a chance because you would never risk losing what you have. Regardless of what takes place in their relationship, their vow of loyalty is a commitment they will never break. "Until death do us part" is written on their hearts as the eleventh commandment! The truth is somewhere in the middle.

Whether your view of monogamy is similar to going on a strict diet or it's something you naturally want depends on a lot of factors, especially your life experience. Generally speaking, the more variety you've had with dating, sexual partners, and long-term and short-term relationships, the more you may view monogamy as a sacrifice for a greater good. You're giving up things you enjoy in order to have what you want most. A person who has led a more sheltered or strict, religious lifestyle with regard to dating, sex, and relationships will find monogamy less of a challenge.

There is a third group of people who demand their mate be monogamous while they allow themselves occasional discrete dalliances. This is the "Do as I say, not as I do" crowd.

In my opinion, monogamy is not natural. It's a lifestyle choice that requires maturity, self-discipline, and an internal moral code that places *honesty* above all other traits in relationship dealings.

Promising versus Committing

Most people promise to be faithful; very few actually commit to it. On the surface, the two types of agreements appear to mean the same thing. But there is a major difference between the two. A promise is to give your word or agree to do something. A commitment implies a stronger obligation, *dedication*, steadfast, and unswerving feat.

Which one of the following sentences implies determination and fortitude?

He promised to see the job through to the end.

He was clearly committed to seeing the job through to the end.

How many times have you heard someone say, "Promises were made to be broken"? But have you ever heard anyone say, "Commitments were made to be broken"? Given a choice between being with someone that promises to be faithful and someone who is committed to being faithful, I'll take the committed person every time! One has to be committed to living a monogamous lifestyle.

Cheating

It's nearly impossible to have a discussion on monogamy without looking at cheating and polygamy. Most people who are married and even those in serious relationships expect monogamy. Naturally there are exceptions, such as couples that have open marriages or a friends-with-benefits arrangement. In both of these instances, having sex with someone outside of their relationship would not be considered cheating.

Cheating is a cowardly, selfish, immature act perpetrated by people who would rather lie, deceive, and hide their desire for a change in a relationship. Cheating requires deception whether it's lying directly or by omission. There is no such thing as an honest cheater. If everything were out it in the open, it would not be called cheating. The very definition of a cheater invokes synonyms such as con artist, swindler, fraud, and impostor. A cheater is someone who *pretends* to be loyal by stating they only want to be with you. He or she tells you how special you are, but behind your back they act as though you don't exist. If you're saying or doing something you would not do with your significant other sitting next to you, there is a good chance you are cheating.

There are countless reasons why people say they cheat: they felt neglected or unappreciated, they were sexually discontent, they fell out of love or wanted revenge, an unusual opportunity presented itself, they never got over an ex, they experienced the thrill of being with someone different while keeping it a secret, or they unexpectedly became emotionally connected with a platonic friend. The mature thing to do when you are unhappy with any aspect of your relationship is to tell the other person what is bothering you or what you would like to see happen. If they are unable or unwilling to give you what you *need*, let them know you are moving on. It requires courage to face problems head on.

Cheating is a selfish act because the cheater wants to keep the things he or she values in the primary relationship while getting something extra on the side. They choose to stay in their marriage or long-term relationship for numerous reasons. Maybe it's financially better to stay. Or maybe there are kids and he or she has no desire to be a weekend parent. A cheater uses the other woman or man to fill a perceived gap in his or her primary relationship. The cheater does not want to deal with the potential repercussions that come with making a choice to be honest.

Although women do cheat in relationships, for the sake of illustration, the next few paragraphs relate to a situation where a man is suspected of cheating. I've read many articles geared toward women concerning signs that indicate whether their man may be cheating. These articles tell them to look for changes in his behavior, such as if he's spending more time away from her, starting fights over the smallest issues, not being where he says he is going to be or with whom he says he is going to be with, or if he is becoming more secretive and emotionally distant.

What is a woman to do? Should you go on a witch-hunt, looking for clues and analyzing his every word, deed, or article of clothing? Do you hire a private detective? Install a keylogger on his computer? Show up at places where he is supposed to be? Look through his cell phone for text messages? Do you install hidden cameras in the house for when you are going to be away? Call the television show *Cheaters*? Do you pester him until he confesses? The answer to all of these questions is no! You cannot control another person. He is going to do whatever he wants to do. The only person responsible for your happiness is you!

Ultimately, it does not matter if your man is cheating! Being cheated on hurts. However, you have no control over what someone else does. The only thing you can do is decide if you want to accept that as the status quo in your relationship. When I say it doesn't matter, what I mean is that if you suspect your mate is cheating, then you must feel something is not right or is *missing* in the relationship. This is causing you alarm. If it turns out that he is not cheating, most likely you still feel as though you are not getting the love, attention, respect, or whatever else is missing that caused you to believe your relationship is not secure. I make no apologies for cheaters, but I think it does nothing for a person to focus on things they have no control over. We are in charge of who we let into our lives. We cannot escape the fact we chose these people.

Hopefully with each bad experience, we learn something about ourselves as well as how to pick better people to associate with. You have to think of yourself as being president and CEO of Me, Inc. Sometimes candidates will show up and give excellent interviews, but once you give them the job, you discover there isn't a match. Life is short. Don't waste too much time trying to force a square peg into a round hole. We have all made mistakes by getting involved with the wrong people. Forgive yourself and promise to do better, and then move on. Your life is the result of choices and decisions *you* make. It's a given that bad things are going to happen to each of us, but it's how we react and what we learn from these circumstances that will determine the quality of our life. If you suspect your significant other is cheating, assume you are right. Even if you are wrong, your sense that you are not in a loving, secure relationship should not be ignored. You are unhappy because something is missing. If you find out he is not cheating, it won't change how you feel about the relationship.

Discovering you are no longer at the top of his priority list hurts almost as much as being betrayed. He may rather spend his free time with friends or family away from you. There are many ways to be cheated on, and they don't all have to do with having sex with someone outside of the relationship. Cheating is having someone take advantage of you or giving you less than what was promised.

There are three basic types of cheaters. They can be male or female.

1. The Incessant Cheater

This person flirts all the time and believes variety is the spice of life. Most likely he or she has never had a monogamous relationship. This person is the typical thrill seeker that bores easily and has a short attention span. He or she is usually outgoing and charismatic. People love being in the company of this person.

2. The Unbelievable Opportunity Cheater

This person is happy with his or her spouse and has no *plans* to cheat, but someone out of his or her league—very attractive, famous, or powerful—made him-or herself available for one night, and the cheater caved in due to temptation. Sometimes it's someone they had a crush on. It's not unusual for this type of cheater to confess months or even years later in order to selfishly remove the burden of guilt from his or her shoulders.

3. The Discontented Cheater

This person feels unloved, unappreciated, and taken for granted or that he or she is not having sexual or emotional needs met. In this person's mind, he or she feels justified or forced to seek out other options to address these needs. Sometimes through no effort of his or her own, a person comes into the discontented partner's life like a ray of sunshine and lifts his or her spirit. The married or attached person was ripe for an affair. It does not take much for a stranger to put a smile on the face and in the heart of a neglected person.

Course of Action

Cheating is a cowardly act perpetrated by those who seek to address a need of some kind. It takes more courage to end an unhappy marriage or relationship than it does to betray someone's trust. Someone's desire to maintain his or her living standard and image can cause him or her to view cheating as a better option than divorce. In all honesty, the only person you can control is yourself. Therefore it is almost impossible to keep someone from cheating on you. Just as monogamy is a choice, so is cheating.

Overcoming the damage of an affair is extremely difficult. In my opinion, coping with the discontented cheater may be slightly easier if the betrayed party concludes they did in fact neglect his or her spouse or ignored pleas for better communication. This by no means excuses the actions of the cheater but rather acknowledges the possibility that one's own behavior contributed to the demise of the relationship. If both people remain in love with one another, couples counseling may be beneficial.

Bigamy Is Cheating on Steroids

Anyone who is secretly married to more than one person at a time is called a bigamist. The word bigamist actually sounds more sophisticated than cheater, but in my opinion this is cheating at its lowest form. Imagine finding out your spouse is married to someone else and has another family. It's more common than you may believe.

There have been many instances where a married foreigner has come to America to attend a university or work a job assignment for a few years and finds him- or herself reaching out to someone out of loneliness. Over time the relationship grows deeper, and for whatever reason a decision is made to get married. Maybe there was an accidental pregnancy, or the foreigner decided to stay in the States and abandon his original family, or he plans to maintain both families by traveling back and forth.

In other instances, military personnel have married or started families while serving in a foreign country, and their original spouses back home have no idea.

Last but not least, we have the domestic bigamist; this person has another spouse or family across town or across the country. Usually a bigamist has a profession that requires a lot of travel or absence from home. This affords him an opportunity to lead a double life with smaller odds of getting caught.

Polygamy Is Not Cheating

Polygamy, like monogamy, is a lifestyle choice accepted under the law in some societies. It dates back prior to biblical times. Each person is aware of the circumstances. In fact, the Bible states in 1 Kings 11:3 that Solomon had seven hundred wives and three hundred concubines! According to 2 Samuel 12:8, God spoke through the prophet Nathan and said that if David's wives and concubines were not enough, he would have given David even more! Exodus 21:10 says, "If he take him another wife; her food, her raiment, and her duty of marriage, shall he not diminish." Essentially this verse is saying if a man can afford multiple wives without reducing the previous wife's benefits, then he is in good standing with God's law.

Some people swear by the Old Testament, and others claim the New Testament is a new covenant and replaces the old. However, the Ten Commandments and other stories still taught from the Bible are found in the Old Testament. The Bible is full of contradictions, and people tend to cherry pick the verses that justify their cause. Whether or not you agree with my interpretation of the Bible's perspective on polygamy, it's clear that it has something to say on the issue.

I wrote the following article to illustrate how a lack of communication and making assumptions about exclusivity can lead to pain.

No Talk, No Ring—Is It Cheating?

When a relationship is undefined, meaning there has been no discussion of exclusivity, and someone *learns* that the person they have been dating is also dating other people, is this cheating? Todd and Amanda met online three months ago. After several e-mail and chat exchanges, they decided to meet. They really clicked and were soon spending lots of time with each other and going to various events, including weekend getaways. On occasion, each of them had other obligations or plans with family or friends.

Two weeks ago, Todd's co-workers talked him into going to a happy hour at the Signature Lounge, located at the top of the John Hancock building in Chicago. He originally wanted to be with Amanda, but she was entertaining a friend from out of town. To his dismay, when he arrived in the lounge, Amanda was sitting in a corner making out with a guy.

Todd caught Amanda's eye and signaled for her to meet him in the hall by the elevators. When Amanda met him, he was very upset and asked her what was going on. Amanda was very taken aback by his manner and in a calm voice stated she was on a date.

She continued, "I told you I was expecting a friend from out of town."

Todd replied, "You never said your friend was a guy!"

"What difference does it make? We never said we were soul mates or exclusive!"

"How would you feel if I took another woman out?"

"Neither one of us is wearing a ring! You can do whatever you want to do."

Amanda walked back to her table, and Todd went home fuming.

Generally speaking, there are two schools of thought. One group believes Todd should have spoken up and told Amanda he wanted an "exclusive relationship" with her a while back. Another group of people believes Amanda was practicing deception or lying by omission when she told Todd she was going to spend time with a friend.

Historically, dating was and still remains for the most part an activity engaged in by two people for the purpose of *assessing* if they are suitable for a long-term relationship. Dating multiple people is akin to a company interviewing several candidates for a position. However, companies inform each candidate they are conducting interviews with others. Candidates never make assumptions they have gotten a position until an offer has been made. They continue to submit their resumes to other companies. When it comes to dating, emotions often arise, which changes the dynamics.

Each of us is entitled to set up our own rules when it comes to dating. If one decides dating multiple people is the way to go, it's probably a good idea in this day and age of numerous STDs to stipulate that if someone is having sex, he or she will either inform the other people they are dating or abstain from having sex altogether.

There is no right or wrong in terms of who is most suitable for each other but simply agree or disagree. Ultimately we are all looking for someone who *naturally agrees* with us.

Communication is always better than assumption.

Would you say Amanda cheated on Todd? Should monogamy be automatically *assumed* after a period of dating? Or is it as Beyoncé stated in her hit song "Single Ladies" that if Todd liked it, he "should have put a ring on it." Is dating more than one person at a time cheating? Or is it actively searching for Mr. or Ms. Right? Would you feel differently if it had been Todd caught with another woman and he responded in the same manner as Amanda?

In response to the article, I got numerous comments stating Amada had not cheated. Some people felt Todd should have told her what he wanted, and some people stated Amanda should have been up front with

Todd about her desire to date others. Still others felt there was a double standard, where many of the women who believed Amanda was not cheating would have felt differently had Todd been caught with a another woman.

The bottom line is, never make assumptions when entering a relationship. Open and honest communication could have prevented this misunderstanding. Just because you spend every weekend together and talk to one another at least once a day does not mean the person you are seeing believes the two of you are exclusive. Unless there is a discussion, promise, or commitment to be monogamous, there are no rules. Some people believe monogamy only applies to engagements or marriage, not dating.

There Is **No Neutral** Gear in **Relationships**

Seasons Change

No truer words were ever spoken than the lyrics of the song "Everything Must Change."

Everything must change

Nothing stays the same

Everyone will change

No one stays the same

Cause that's the way of time

Nothing and no one goes unchanged

—Benard Ighner

In any long-term relationship, you are either growing together or growing apart. Change is inevitable. Hopefully throughout the course of one's life, there are periods of evolvement. Those messages written in your high school yearbook by your peers such as "Don't ever change…" were not meant to keep your wisdom at the level of an eighteen-year-old. Our desires and goals change from time to time. Nothing is written in stone. Life is fluid, and therefore we're likely to change directions now and then. With experience comes wisdom and growth.

When we start off in life, we adopt many of our parent's ideas about how to live. This may entail everything from grocery products we purchase as adults to how we vote in elections. Most of us venture into other directions over time as we form our own opinions. Eventually we adopt our own philosophy based upon our own experiences in life. In essence, we redefine ourselves.

This evolutionary process never completely stops. It affects everything we desire in life, including the type of mate we select. A teenage girl may be interested in meeting a cute boy that makes her laugh and is popular among her classmates. The same young lady attending college may want to connect with a guy based upon his ambition and career prospects. At a different stage in her life, she might desire a man who is more romantic, family oriented, and grounded. It's possible one boy could grow into being all of these men. Down the road, this same woman may decide to swear off men altogether! As mentioned earlier, nothing is written in stone.

Ideally a couple has the same goals regarding the future of their relationship. If one of them should change their mind, he or she would communicate a change of heart and propose a new direction. Surprisingly, more often than not, their significant other is also ready to go in a new direction. It just took one of them to speak up. A couple that continues to want the same things at the same pace are growing together. In contrast, a couple that has radical differences of opinion as to how to approach their future is growing apart.

Life Happens

Not every change is predicated by an individual's choice or desire. It's possible to know what you want in a relationship, pursue a person in agreement with you, and wake up one day to find life has changed your circumstances.

When Gary met Michelle, he was forty-two and she was forty-eight. Gary lived in an apartment on a beach in Southern California, and Michelle lived approximately thirty miles away. Michelle had an adult daughter that she was sharing a two-bedroom apartment with. On most weekends, Michelle would drive up to Gary's place. Their weekends together were full of passion, laughter, food, wine, and evening strolls along the shore. Gary and Michelle traveled up and down the coast from San Diego to San Francisco and to several other destinations, such as Las Vegas, New York, Seattle, New Orleans, Chicago, Hawaii, and beyond.

Initially when they began seeing each other, Michelle was always a blast to be around. She was the type of person that made friends easily. Michelle was passionate and always ready to have some fun. She wanted to get to the party early and be the last one to leave. Gary observed she sometimes would drink too much, especially around her close friends. She clowned around a little too much for his liking. This often made him the designated driver and surrogate parent when he was forced to tell her it was time to go.

In her day-to-day life, Michelle was a hardworking legal secretary with a big heart. She was generous to family, friends, and strangers. Michelle wanted everyone to be happy. Looking back, I guess one could say she fit the classic middle child pleaser profile. Many of these traits made her irresistible to Gary.

Their first year together was like that of many couples who find new love. They cruised through the infatuation phase, had some disagreements, and eventually settled into the attachment phase of their relationship. Gary relocated to be closer to his job, which was also closer to Michelle. After two years of spending nights at each other's apartments, they found a place to live together. As a couple they'd visit her family, friends, and attend each other's company events.

Michelle had three daughters. Sarah, the oldest, lived in Northern California with her husband. Dawn, the middle daughter, was a teacher, and Paula, the youngest, worked in a local grocery store and also waited tables for an Italian restaurant.

Gary was the product of divorced parents. He had two slightly younger brothers who had relocated from the Midwest to California, just like he had. Neither Gary nor his brothers had ever wanted to have children. In fact Gary had gotten a vasectomy several years prior. He cherished the freedom that came with being childless. His mother along with most of his relatives lived two thousand miles away. Gary's friends were his family for the most part. His life was debt free, carefree, and drama free.

The Winds of Change

Like most things in life, change often begins in small degrees but eventually amounts to a major shift. Sarah and her husband moved to Southern California. Once they got settled, they began to have kids. Naturally, this was a joyous occasion for Michelle and her ex-husband. The birth of grandchildren led to more family events with her ex and former in-laws. Gary and Michelle would baby-sit from time to time.

Family Illness

Around this same time, Michelle's mother was diagnosed with cancer in her intestines. After surgery it was necessary for her to sell her condo and move into a nursing home. The first year her mother was there, Michelle went to visit her every evening after work, and on weekends Gary would often accompany her. Sometimes they would take her mom out of the home for dinners or to visit with other family members.

After the first year, Michelle began cutting back on visits to the nursing home by going every other day. On her free evenings, sometimes she went straight home; other times she went out for happy hour cocktails with co-workers or had dinner with girlfriends. A few times Gary had to go pick Michelle up because she had drunk too much to drive.

There were also times when Michelle found herself feuding with her own siblings over their mother's care. This was another source of stress for her.

Family Drama

Paula, Michelle's youngest daughter, purchased a condo where she met and fell in love with Tom, a fellow owner. Soon after their relationship began, Tom became verbally abusive and gradually became physically abusive, slapping her, spitting on her, and threatening her. One night, Paula dropped by Gary and Michelle's home. She revealed detail after detail regarding her relationship with Tom as she cried her eyes out. Paula lay in the middle of the kitchen floor in a fetal position as Michelle cried and rocked her. Paula spent the next couple of nights with them until Tom called her begging for forgiveness. This was only the start of their abusive, yo-yo relationship.

Dawn, the middle child, earned over forty thousand dollars a year as a teacher and had a one-bedroom apartment. For some reason she was always broke, which led her to call Michelle for money from time to time. Although Michelle had her own mountain of debt, she always came through like a hero for Dawn. Each year before school began, Michelle took Dawn shopping to buy her clothes.

Dawn did not take responsibility for her financial woes. Instead she was resentful of her older sister, Sarah, who had a master's degree but never worked because she had met and fell in love with a guy from a rich family while attending college. In Dawn's eyes, Sarah was handed everything on a silver platter, and now that she had given the family grandchildren, everyone was fawning over her.

Bye-Bye Passionate Sex Life

Michelle had begun to experience menopause symptoms. Her sexual desire faded, and she was not concerned with pleasing Gary anymore. Sex was erratic at best and completely without imagination or creativity. Even when they managed to have a getaway, more often than not there was no sex.

Most weekends involved Gary and Michelle going to visit her family or friends or hosting a barbecue. During the week, Michelle visited her mother, socialized with girlfriends, or had drinks with co-workers. Weeks turned into months, and months turned into years.

Let Freedom Ring

One Saturday afternoon, Gary stood alone before a smoky hot grill, cooking chicken and hot links while Michelle's family was in the cool indoors talking, laughing, and listening to music. The grandchildren were running up and down the stairs screaming, laughing, and turning lights on and off. Toys were strewn all over the house. Sarah had just delighted the family by announcing she was pregnant with her third child.

As Gary stood before the grill, he thought back to the life he used to have six and a half years prior. He realized how much he missed the life he had. He also knew if he stayed in this relationship, nothing was going to change for the better. After attending his first "potty party" to celebrate a child's first use of the toilet, he quietly asked himself, "How did I get here?" Gary knew what he had to look forward to by staying in this relationship. There would be more family gatherings, more drama, less one-on-one time with Michelle, and less sex. In many ways, Gary had become invisible in his own home.

He felt like he was being taken for granted and unappreciated. Nothing spoke louder to him than Michelle forgetting to buy him a simple Christmas card that year. As he began to place the chicken and hot links on a platter, Michelle stuck her head outdoors and said, "Are we done?"

Gary looked up from the grill and replied, "Yes, we're done."

Meet My Current Life Partner

Serial Monogamy

A serial monogamist lives life on repeat. Commitment for him or her is being in one relationship at a time. It's not about being with one person for life. This type of person throws his or her heart into the ring without establishing anything close to the basic fundamentals required to have a truly happy and long-lasting relationship. It's not unheard of to hear him or her proclaim they are in love after dating a person for eight weeks or less! But it takes longer than two months to *really* get to know someone.

The Infatuation Phase

Everything is new, exciting, fun, and the couple's focus is only on the things they have in common. Sex is passionate and unpredictable. Laughter comes easily and often. Every weekend feels like a romantic weekend getaway or mini vacation. Making each other happy is their number-one priority.

One day while the couple is taking a stroll along the shore, having breakfast, lounging after sex, or simply waking up next to one another, one of them whispers, "I love you."

Ninety-nine percent of the time, the other person *automatically* responds by saying, "I love you too."

Once those words have been uttered, you can't take them back without coming across as a liar, a manipulator, or a fickle person. Every action, word, or deed going forward must exemplify and illustrate your deep devotion for this person. Any contradiction between your words and your behavior will lead to negative consequences. Unfortunately, nothing stays *new* forever!

The Attachment Phase

At this point in a relationship, typically there have been some strong disagreements. Imperfections in each person have been discovered. Both people have disappointed one another in some way, but the good times still outnumber the bad or uneasy times. This is the phase where terms such as "communication issues" and "relationship work" come into play. Each person struggles to determine if it's worth it to fight for the relationship. Those that stick it out will continue to experience elements of the "infatuation phase" at times.

Attachment is acceptance of an imperfect life together.

The Breakup Phase

A final straw or "deal breaker" has occurred, and someone in the relationship realizes they are unable to live with the way things are and cannot imagine things getting better in the future. Quite often at this point someone has fallen completely out of love. The two people's goals are no longer aligned.

The relationship or marriage has evolved into a parent-child union or roommates with the same last name. A list of reasons as to why people break up could go on for eternity. Whatever the reason, one person has determined their life would be better off without their significant other in it. Now it becomes a matter of choosing a way to exit the relationship.

The Indirect Approach

This approach involves forcing the other person to break up with them. This is done by intentionally doing things that irritate him or her. One example is allowing him- or herself to be caught flirting, cheating, or doing something that disrespects the relationship. Either of these can easily push a mate over the top.

This type of person prefers to let the partner *believe* they ended the relationship. This approach cuts down on a lot of the heavy drama elements in a typical breakup. The reason there is less drama is due to the lack of surprise by the person being dumped. After all, he or she orchestrated the scenario. All the one being dumped has to do is articulate they understand and say, "I hope we can remain friends."

Shockingly, there are times the indirect approach does not work. This happens when the wronged person is willing to *forgive* and continue with the relationship! This person is determined to stay in a relationship no matter how bad it gets. A situation like this typically forces the serial monogamist to communicate his or her desire to split.

The Direct Approach

This approach involves sitting down at an appropriate time to state one's plans to exit the relationship. One of the challenges with this approach is its unpredictability. Even when there has been a difficult time in a relationship, it still may come as a shock to the person being dumped. A wide range of emotions could be displayed: uncontrolled anger, loud crying as if wounded, accusations of infidelity, and in extreme cases, violence.

Often a person caught off guard attempts to manipulate the conversation away from breaking up into a *negotiation session*, as if your intentions were to issue an ultimatum instead of declaring the relationship is over. Most of us have been dumped in one form or another. Whether it was being laid off from a job or having your heart broken, begging or watching someone else beg is a terrible sight.

The Cowardly Approach

This is also known as the non confrontational approach. A person secretly plans and executes his or her exit, all the while behaving as if everything were going fine. He or she spends free time looking for an apartment, setting aside money, and slowly packing his or her things. One day this person calls in sick, loads up the car, and leaves his or her significant other a note. Other variations of this method include e-mailing, texting, or leaving a voice mail when they know the other person is unable to answer the phone. A debate rages on as to what is the best or worst way to break up with someone. Most people place themselves in the shoes of the person being let go and not the initiator.

Good-bye Is Good-bye

From my perspective, there is no right or wrong way to end a relationship. The method used is at the discretion and comfort level of the person ending the relationship. We don't get to tell someone how and when to dump us. It comes down to the type of relationship and personalities involved. A woman in a household with domestic violence is probably better off taking the cowardly approach. No one expects to be hurt or killed because of a breakup but it does happen on occasion. Ultimately the person who is doing the dumping will do so in a manner most comfortable for him or her. None of us has a say in how we are to be let go from a job or a relationship. It's audacious and arrogant to think otherwise.

Closure is a word often thrown around when a relationship has run its course. If you are being dumped, there is nothing your former partner can say to you that will unbreak your heart. You are better off accepting things are over and moving on. I've heard some people state they want to know why so that they might work on themselves to improve things in a future relationship. However, the very thing that caused their ex to leave them may be the same thing that causes another person to fall madly in love with them. No matter the reason, your ex has determined his or her life would be happier or better without you in it. The following contains an article I wrote concerning closure.

"It's Not You; It's Me": Is Closure Really Important?

Recently I read a letter written to an advice columnist, which detailed a relationship that ended after three years. The man in this relationship asked the woman why she was dumping him, and she told him, "It's not you; it's me." When he pressed her, he got more of what he termed "evasive answers." He now questions if she was ever in love with him. He wanted to know how one could tell if his or her mate was really in love.

Naturally the columnist assured him he would find true love with someone who felt the same way about him as he does for them. The letter got me to wondering, what is the upside to knowing why you were dumped? Will getting closure ease your pain or change your reality?

I posted the following comment in reply to the advice column.

Closure Is Overrated

All you really need to know is this person no longer wants to be with you. Asking them questions only puts them on the spot. If they're kind, they will naturally tell you things such as "It's not you; it's me."

Would you rather they say, "It's you! Your breath stinks! I hate your friends! Sex with you is boring! I'm tired of hearing you snore!" Would that really make you feel better?

One reason people end relationships saying, "It's not you; it's me" is because they know if they gave you a list of reasons, chances are you would beg them to stay.

Some examples are saying such things as:

I'll change! I'll brush my teeth three times a day!

I'll drop my friends. I'll buy you the Rabbit vibrator.

I'll wear Breathe Right nose strips before we go to sleep.

Listening to someone beg, watching them drop their self-dignity, crying and pleading while knowing in your heart there is nothing they can say or do that would cause you to stay creates an ugly, messy scene. Several months later, if you were the one begging, you'd end up kicking yourself for behaving like that.

When someone tells you "It's me not you," that's the truth! They want to move on. They want to see someone else. They feel they can do better, love deeper, and have more joy without you in their life. You, on the other hand, are content with things as they are. They had a change of heart, and you didn't.

My guess is that during the course of your three-year relationship, there were changes that took place along the way. There were clues or signs that she wasn't as emotionally invested in the relationship as you were. Maybe it was always *you* making the first move to mend fences after a disagreement. Maybe it was always *you* who made a big deal out of anniversaries, birthdays, and holidays. Maybe it was *you* that came up with the special date ideas or romantic getaway suggestions. Maybe it was *you* that sprung the surprise gifts and gave greeting cards or love notes "just because."

Sometimes we are so much in love that we neglect to see how very little love is actually being given back to us. We mistake the crumbs that are tossed our way for a whole cake.

Love is not about keeping score, but if someone is in love with you there, should be too many wonderful things they have said, done, or given that makes it impossible for you to count.

Accept It When It's Over

Asking for closure at the end of relationship is often akin to asking to be slapped or kicked in the head as the person walks out the door.

There is nothing your ex can say that will make you feel better about having your heart broken.

Life as a serial monogamist is mentally, physically, and emotionally exhausting. Developing love and devotion over time, after a solid foundation has been established, creates a much better chance for having a relationship that will endure.

Syntax Matters
When Baking
Love

The Recipe for Relationship Happiness

There are basic ingredients in all recipes. Many of us might elect to add our own twist making them more suitable to our palate. However there are some ingredients that if removed simply don't add up to the ideal dish. You would be hard pressed to make a great pound cake without flour or lasagna without pasta. These items are among the basic ingredients required to make those dishes.

It's not enough to know the ingredients of a recipe. It is important to know the syntax, or order, of things. When you mix ingredients in a different order, you get a slightly different result. If you leave one ingredient out or substitute one, you also get something else. There is always more than one way to make an entrée. Both KFC and Popeye's serve fried chicken with completely different recipes. Naturally they both start off with chicken and flour, but the spices they use vary tremendously.

In the same way, I believe the foundation of any happy marriage or relationship is built upon the following six building blocks, or ingredients. These blocks could also be thought of as chain links with each coming into existence and getting stronger because of the previous one.

1. Honesty leads to trust

2. Trust leads to loyalty

3. Loyalty leads to love and devotion

4. Love and devotion lead to intimacy

5. Intimacy leads to emotional security

6. Emotional security leads to real happiness

And real happiness is what makes life worth living! Every relationship I have been in that has failed, I can point to at least one and more often two or three blocks that were missing. Honesty is the most important building block of them all.

Honesty

A relationship without honesty is equivalent to building a house on sand or without a foundation. It is not going to last. The truth will eventually come out, or the liar becomes bored with making a fool out of his or her mate and decides to move on. Everyone is quick to say communication is the key to a happy relationship. It should be said *honest communication* is a key to a happy relationship.

If someone will lie about insignificant things, you know they will lie about major things, especially if the truth reflects negatively on them. The purpose of a lie is to *control or manipulate* the reactions of the person listening. Liars are selfish by nature and will say anything to get their way, especially if they believe it will make their lives easier. They don't concern themselves with what may happen if the truth should come out because they don't believe they will get caught. All cheaters and con men are liars whose intent is to win over your confidence and trust.

There are two basic reasons why people lie:

1. To avoid the pain or repercussions of dealing with the truth. This includes causing someone else pain and dealing with their anger, hurt, and disappointment. Liars lack the courage to be honest with the people they lie to. Most liars have a problem being honest with themselves as well.

2. To keep the thrill alive. Whatever they are doing behind your back, they don't want to stop. Therefore they lie to avoid being pressured to stop.

When someone lies to you, it may cause you to feel insulted as well as hurt. It is especially painful when a lie comes from your spouse, best friend, or someone else that you have placed your trust in. This causes you to re-examine everything they have ever said. The more lies they have told you, the more questions you have. I do, however, believe that trust can be rebuilt if the person who has lied sincerely regrets telling the lie instead of simply being upset that they were caught in a lie. It will require extra effort on his or her part to be transparent in both words and deeds.

Three Steps to Rebuilding Trust

The following steps can be used for restoring a relationship that has been damaged through dishonesty.

Offer a genuine apology and promise not to lie again. Don't attempt to justify the lie or offer an excuse for the lie. To do so only implies that given a similar circumstance, you would lie again. Admit that you betrayed the person's trust and reassure them it won't happen again.

Acknowledge it will take some time to earn the person's complete trust but assure him or her you are determined to do so. State that you will be both understanding and patient when they have questions from time to time regarding your actions or things you may have told them.

Strive to live your life in such a way that you think beyond yourself and consider what is in the best interest for your relationship.

After having this discussion, you must learn to think before you commit an act that could be deemed as a betrayal of his or her trust.

The reason so many people are dishonest and live without integrity is because it takes *courage* to consistently tell truth. Living a life committed to honesty means being willing to risk not being liked. However, it is important not to confuse being honest and direct with being rude or insensitive. The truth is often ugly or hurtful and can lead to dire consequences. It's human nature for a person to seek to avoid pain or being placed in a tense situation. This explains why there are so many liars.

In order to have the best outcome in any form of communication, it is always wise to utilize your mental edit button before opening your mouth or typing. It takes courage to give your heart completely to one person and to let someone get to know the *real you*. It takes courage to tell the truth and ask for forgiveness. It takes even more courage to forgive and give someone a second chance. When someone fills your head and heart with beautiful words that contradict their behavior, it is almost impossible to add the next link in the relationship chain.

Trust

You cannot build trust without honesty being firmly established. Trust is based upon both people in the relationship demonstrating honesty and integrity. Trust is very similar to respect in that it should be *earned* over time. It is not something to be given away lightly. We tell our children not to talk to strangers because they are not to be trusted. Later in life, as adults, many of us adopt the opposite philosophy. I've heard several people say, "I'll trust anyone until they prove me wrong." This way of thinking is a conman's dream!

We live in a time where it's not politically correct to state a gullible person bears some responsibility for being taking advantage of. I have heard the following statement said with regard to rape victims: "I don't care if a woman walks down an alley butt naked at two in the morning. No one has the right to rape her." I completely agree with that statement. No one has the right! I would also say, "It's not a *wise* thing for a woman to walk the streets naked." There are many things people generally know to do in order to prevent theft or other harm. For example:

It is not smart for a woman to leave her purse on the roof of her car overnight.

It is not smart for a man to leave his wallet on a park bench.

It is not wise to sleep with the doors to your house wide open.

It probably is not a good idea to walk down a street counting your money.

It probably is not a good idea to leave your keys in the ignition of your car overnight.

Doing any of the above actions does not constitute giving someone the right or permission to take advantage of you. However, we cannot ignore our obligation to look out for ourselves. No one has a more vested interest to look out for you!

Pedestrians have the right-of-way, and yet we tell children to look both ways before crossing the street! We don't step out into the street assuming everyone is going to see us and obey the law. The primary responsibility of any parent is to prepare his or her child for adulthood by teaching the child to think and to look out for him- or herself.

Ask Me No Questions

Some people are of the mindset if you trust them you shouldn't question them. However, in reality, trust is not about withholding questions you may have for your partner. Trust comes as a result of asking questions and getting straightforward answers in return. In fact, I would say trouble is lurking if you are in a relationship with someone you cannot ask questions of. Trust is your instinctive reaction to what was said or done. Trust may also be employed in anticipation of having our expectations met. These expectations are based upon past experiences we have had with the individual.

A person in love with you wants to assure you that you have nothing to worry about. Anyone who gives you quick answers to shut you up and send you on your way, answers your question with a question, becomes loud or indignant, calls you paranoid, or takes offense to you asking questions is probably not concerned about what you think. To ask someone a question is nothing more than searching for understanding. The questioner wants to avoid making assumptions. Trust is based upon facts given to us. An assumption is a hypothetical guess.

A Call from No One

Amy and John are driving along the highway. John's cell phone rings. He looks at the incoming number and decides to ignore it.

Amy asks, "Who was that?"

"No one."

The phone makes a noise indicating a message has been left.

Amy prompts "Aren't you going to check your voice mail?"

"I can do it later on."

"Why not check it now?"

"Because I don't feel like it! What's up with all the questions? You sound like you don't trust me."

"I trust you. I was just wondering why you didn't want to take the call. That's all."

John explodes. "It's my phone, and I can answer it whenever I get good and damn ready! You need to get over your trust issues and stop being so paranoid."

Amy reclines in her seat and closes her eyes as if she is going to sleep.

Throughout the whole conversation, John didn't give Amy any information about the call. He began by being evasive, and when that did not stop her from inquiring further, he went into anger mode to shut her up. Asking questions does not always signify trust issues. However, *refusing* to answer questions usually creates trust issues.

After an exchange such as this, it should come as no surprise if Amy decided to look at John's phone when he fell asleep or snoop through his cell phone statements. Trust is not about taking anything for granted, assuming, or feeling obligated to give someone the benefit of the doubt. It's not about keeping quiet when you have questions.

Trust is a belief you have been given an honest answer to your questions!

Based upon information we are given, we determine whether or not it's trustworthy. Actions, words, or deeds that display honesty and integrity precede the act of trusting. Never let anyone belittle you for asking questions. A cheater believes, "If you trusted me, you wouldn't have busted me." When someone loves you, they want to reassure you, put your mind at ease, and leave no room for doubt that you are very important to them. They would never intentionally harm you. Knowing someone is on your side creates loyalty, the next building block.

Loyalty

"Through thick and through thin, come hell or high water, I've got your back!"

Simply hearing those words from a loved one can lift your spirits no matter what obstacles in life you may be facing. Knowing you have somewhere to land should you fall is a safety net you can't put a price on. Loyalty evokes other words such as commitment, dependable, and trustworthy.

In a way, the exchange of wedding vows is nothing more than a promise to be loyal in sickness and good health, until death do you part, and so forth in front of witnesses. It's an announcement to the world that your mate can count on you, and vice versa.

There is no loyalty without honesty and trust. One must let go of jealousy, however.

The Green-Eyed Monster
Upon arriving at the newest chic restaurant in town, Scott and Linda were greeted by the maitre d'. He

shook Scott's hand, and when he took Linda's hand he leaned forward and kissed it while saying, "We are truly honored to have such a beautiful madam dinning with us tonight." Linda smiled broadly and batted her eyes uncontrollably. Once they were seated, Linda noticed a scowl on Scott's face as he stared intently at the menu.

Linda asked, "What's the matter?"

"I didn't like the way you gushed all over the place a few minutes ago."

In another situation, Bill and Mary are seated at a table as a party gets underway.

A beautiful woman approaches them and she asks Mary if it would be okay to borrow Bill to hold a ladder while she pulled some things down from a high shelf. Bill stands up and begins to walk.

Mary mumbles, "I wish I could get you to move that fast to help me."

Both of the preceding scenarios are examples of jealousy.

The compliment paid to Linda and the request for Bill's assistance was *unsolicited*. They did nothing to draw attention to themselves. Nonetheless, the remarks made by their partners would imply they did something wrong.

Jealousy is known as the "green-eyed monster." It can rear its ugly head without warning. Unlike betrayal, the act causing jealousy is rarely an actual threat to the relationship. Instead of feeling fortunate to have a mate other people admire and quite possibly desire, the jealous person becomes insecure.

There are individuals who enjoy getting a reaction from their significant other by deliberately doing things to cause him or her to become jealous. Their goal is to get more attention from their partner whom they feel is neglecting them. In extreme cases, a jealous person may become controlling or violent in order to discourage his or her partner from drawing unwanted attention. Another tactic sometimes used by a jealous person is to have sex with someone outside of their relationship in an effort to boost their own self-esteem. They resent playing second fiddle to their mates and need to feel desired. This might explain the behavior of Halle Berry's ex-husband Eric Benet as well as Sandra Bullock's ex-husband Jesse James.

Betrayal

Betrayal is an intentional act, which violates the understanding, trust, and loyalty thought to be established in a relationship. Unlike jealousy, there is no such thing as incidental or secondary betrayal. A woman who learns her husband has been soliciting a prostitute is not jealous of his relationship with the hooker. She is hurt and devastated by his betrayal.

Love and Devotion

You have been dating someone for a while. Honesty, trust, and loyalty are the foundation of your relationship. It's time to take the most courageous step of all; opening your heart and completely offering your significant other all the love and devotion he or she can handle. Putting your heart and soul into anything is always scary, and this is especially true when it comes to relationships. No matter how much you prepare, there is always a risk of failure, disappointment, and heartbreak.

Insecurity versus Vulnerability

Insecurity comes from doubting your own instincts and not trusting decisions you have made regarding people and situations in your past. In essence, insecurity is having a lack of self-confidence. The only solution for insecurity is to learn from your past mistakes and trust and believe that you are wiser now. With each minor success, your confidence will grow. However, it is a good idea to avoid becoming too emotionally attached to certain results, whether good or bad. I once heard former NBA coach Phil Jackson say: "Don't let success go to your head, and don't let failure go to your heart."

Vulnerability, on the other hand, is about being brave enough to put yourself out there on center stage completely naked, realizing you may be condemned, appreciated, loved or attacked. Giving someone your whole heart, body, trust, and not holding anything back is what being completely in love is all about. It's flying higher than you ever thought possible. It also is the most vulnerable position a person can ever be in!

The very thought of love not being returned or being betrayed is too devastating to think about. It can actually make a person physically ill, and in more extreme cases, even suicidal! In the words of Elvis, "Wise men say only fools fall in love." Not many people are willing to risk it all to have it all. No one wants to be a fool.

We live in a society that teaches us not to love completely. We're taught to hold something back just in case and to keep our options open because you never know. Protecting ourselves is deemed more important than giving of ourselves. Some people keep one foot out of the relationship door by seeing other people on the side, flirting, emotionally cheating, or finding other ways to avoid complete intimacy with one person. Oftentimes they sabotage an opportunity to experience the greatest gift this world has to offer, the deepest love possible.

For many people, avoiding the deepest level of devotion and love also means avoiding pain. The most insecure people in the world are those who lack the courage to be vulnerable enough to fall in love. They are too afraid of actually needing someone. Their cynical side overrides their romantic side. They believe needing someone is a sign of weakness. Each of us nonetheless dreams of being the center of someone else's world. We want someone who will spoil us emotionally and physically. We want a person who genuinely cares about us deeply, someone we can count on day or night—a person who listens to us and at times will put our wants and needs above their own. We want the kind of love that many of us are unwilling or unable to give. One of the most cynical pieces of advice I have ever heard is: "Never marry someone you love. Marry someone who loves you!" I can only assume the person who said it adopted this position in order to protect himself from being hurt.

To be in love is to be vulnerable, and to be vulnerable is to be courageous. Courageous people are willing to take risks to get what they want. Love is a living, breathing emotion capable of growing or retreating. Wanting to know where you stand is not a sign of being insecure. It's an admission to your mate you are vulnerable. Questions arise when a mate changes his or her behavior towards us. If we are not taking our significant other for granted or making assumptions, it is only natural to need a little reassurance from time to time. Communication, affection, passion, and consideration are the keys of reassurance.

The previous links in the chain are in a particular syntax as to minimize the heartache risk. Putting the cart before the horse can lead to learning a painful lesson. Take it from me, starting off with intimacy and attempting to work your way backwards seldom works.

Intimacy

It seems like the longer couples are together, the less intimate they are. Oddly enough, in many ways you would think it would be the opposite since the longer you are with someone, the more you *know* what things they like, how they like to be touched, favorite foods, what makes them happy, sad, or angry, and so forth. As the old adage states, "Practice makes perfect."

Although it is important for one to have his or her own interest growing in this journey we call life, it is far more important to make sure you are not being neglectful to the one person you have taken a vow to become one with. Life, after all, is about balance. A woman should wake up daily and go to bed nightly knowing she is the most important person in her man's life and vice versa. If something doesn't seem right or feel right when you are together, get it out in the open. As the song goes,

"When something is wrong with my baby, something is wrong with me." Ignoring problems is the best way to grow them. Communication is a key to a successful relationship when both people still give a damn about each other's feelings. Honest communication is a requirement.

Intimacy means different things to different people, but essentially it comes down to feeling emotionally connected. It's about sharing your life with someone. This includes your fears, hopes, and dreams in ways you don't share with most people. Intimacy is also about being physically connected. Although sex and its frequency are extremely important in this regard, it is also very important to be physically connected outside of the bedroom throughout the day. This is easily accomplished by doing such things as kissing each other good morning, good-night, good-bye, and hello. Make sure some of those kisses are *wet ones* too. Rubbing each other's shoulders or feet at the end of a day, snuggling together while watching television, playing tricks on one another or trying to make each other laugh, and holding hands while riding in a car are just a few ways of staying physically connected.

End every phone conversation by saying "I love you," because one day it may be the last thing your partner hears you say. Tomorrow is not promised to any man. Saying "I love you" doesn't take much time or energy. Make sure you say it with meaning.

Having one-on-one time together is very important. This can include going out to dinner, a play, a concert, a movie, or a weekend getaway, or doing whatever you did together when you were courting. If money is tight, you can still be intimate by running errands together, shopping, cooking a meal together, watching a DVD, or having discussions about something you read or heard. Asking your mate for his or her opinion also shows you value them.

It can be as simple as having them help you make a decision about something that is happening in your life (e.g., at work or dealing with a friend or family member). Intimacy can also be accomplished through romantic gestures such as mailing your mate a greeting card or love letter without a return address on it, leaving a naughty voice mail on his or her cell phone, tucking a note in with the person's lunch, or leaving a loving message at the office. If you know your mate will arrive home before you, leave them a voice mail on your home answering machine. These gestures take less than a minute each to execute.

Sexual Intimacy

Mutual sexual pleasure should be the goal in any intimate relationship but especially so in a marriage. This means showing and telling your partner ways to excite or turn you on. You must trust your spouse will not judge you for what you say, do, or want done in bed. Your bedroom is your sanctuary, and what happens in there has nothing to do with how you function in the outside world. Sex can become routine if you aren't careful, that is, if you always have it at the same time of day or night of the week, the same location, or the same position, and so forth. Many couples fall into a habit of having one or two go-to moves when it comes to sex. You can spice things up by having it at different times of the day. It is important to have sex in different ways, not just different positions.

Have romantic sex (soft music, wine, and candlelight) in the bedroom or on the floor in front of the fireplace after dinner.

Have erotic sex. Use four letter words, scratch, spank, bite, scream, yell instructions like "faster" or "harder," or tell your mate how good his or her body feels. Let him or her know you are about to climax. You could role play, use toys, massage each other with oils, watch an adult DVD together, and so on. You are only limited by your imagination.

Have spontaneous quickie sex somewhere—no place is safe! Have sex in the shower, in the kitchen, in your car while parked in your garage, in the basement, or on the sofa while watching television.

Be proactive in reaching your orgasms. It is up to you to make sure you have them. If you are a woman, there is nothing wrong with rubbing your clitoris as your man thrusts you from behind. If you are a man, there is nothing wrong with you stroking your penis as your woman gives you oral pleasure. Sexual frustration comes from not reaching orgasms on a regular basis, and if you allow it to go unchecked, after a while one person will come to feel as though he or she is doing their mate a favor. The best time to talk about sexual needs is outside of the bedroom because it takes the pressure out of it.

When you think about it, we spend very few waking hours with our spouses. The majority of our time is spent sleeping or driving to and from work. Many of us bring work home. We also work on pet projects and hobbies or take a nap once we do come home. That does not leave much opportunity for quality time or intimate time.

If couples are not careful, they can effectively end up becoming roommates with the same last name or something akin to siblings. Intimacy is being in touch with the person you love physically, mentally, and emotionally. It means being considerate by calling to let your mate know you are coming home later than usual or if your plans change during the course of the day. It's being the one person your mate can count on to be there in times of need; you are a soft place to fall, his or her best friend, and always honest. If we are not careful, it is easy to go a day, a week, or more without kissing, hugging, holding hands, having sex, or even saying, "I love you." Eventually intimate connection fades to a point where touching only occurs prior to sex.

By this point, complaints come more easily than compliments. Withdrawal may begin with having conflicting schedules or being unable to spend quality time together, going to bed or rising at different times, watching television in separate rooms, eating meals at different times, and being unwilling to make time to carry on any significant conversation. Priorities may have changed to a point where there is always something more important than spending time together. Whenever there is some free time available it is spent at a boy's night out or girl's night out or entertaining family and friends. For many people, it's as if once they have found a mate, they check it off their life to-do list. They don't realize relationships are living entities that require nurturing to grow, and just like plants, if they aren't nurtured, they die. The real secret to increasing intimacy is setting aside time to be alone together.

Emotional Security

When one thinks of the word *security*, it means your needs are taken care of come what may. It's very similar to having auto insurance, homeowner insurance, and health insurance in the event something dire occurs. You are fully aware assistance is available to help you recover. It's natural to feel shaken in response to a natural disaster. However, knowing there is a measure of protection in place gives you some peace of mind.

An emotionally secure person has a support system as well as a positive outlook on life. They are able to make adjustments and keep rolling when they are thrown off track. In order to obtain emotional security, it's important to maintain a well-balanced life. This would entail having family, friends, and co-workers you can lean on for support during rough times. The support is not necessarily financial, but it can be. Primarily it's the type of support that lifts you up mentally and spiritually during difficult times.

Your spouse or partner in life should be an integral part of your support team. This is the person sleeping next to you each night and waking up with you each morning. They have made a commitment to walk with you side by side through life's ups and downs. There is no person closer physically or emotionally as your mate. In a healthy relationship, this person will be the first shoulder you cry on and your sounding board for all the thoughts and feelings swirling through your mind and heart during difficult times.

Being in an emotionally secure relationship means you feel safe to open up about anything without being judged or criticized for how you may be feeling. It's impossible to have emotional security in a relationship without having the previous ingredients covered earlier in this chapter. It's easier to attain happiness when you know that no matter what happens, you will be fine. Having peace of mind allows you to focus on growing into the person you want to be. You're able to take some calculated risks knowing you will be fine because you have an emotionally secure foundation to rely upon.

That's *my basic recipe* for relationship happiness. Feel free to spice it up and add whatever suits your taste. Bon appétit!

With Truth
Comes Clarity

Living in Black and White

When we experience a moment of serendipity or a sudden epiphany, the gray fades away. Answers to puzzling questions we have been trying to solve for ages flow to us easily. We wonder why we were ever perplexed to begin with. Knowing what to do and following through feels exhilarating after being stymied. Clarity puts everything in black and white. We sleep better. There's a sudden boost of energy, and depression gives way to positive thoughts. This occurs even if the problem has yet to be resolved. It is as if by simply having a *strategy* or *plan of attack* to deal with a problem, it becomes less formidable.

Wisdom and clarity are often in abundance when it comes to assisting others with their problems. Perhaps it's because we are not emotionally attached to the problem. We may have already faced the same issue in the past or we know of someone who has had to deal with similar circumstances. Whatever the reason, most of us seem to have no problem dispensing sound advice to others.

Perception Is Reality

Sometimes we are so mired in our problems that we cannot imagine a way out. It eats at us mentally and upsets us physically. We lose sleep while looking for an escape route to avoid facing issues. Some folks opt for alcohol, drugs, sex, food, or lavish spending sprees in order to take their minds off of problems. With each passing day, their problems seem to magnify and a feeling of hopelessness descends upon them. In the worst cases, some people choose suicide.

Different Perceptions of the Same Problem

A five-year-old boy facing an eight-year-old bully believes he is in a life or death situation. Whenever he sees the enemy, his heart races, his palms sweat, his body shakes involuntary, and his breathing becomes shallow and quickens as he looks for an escape route.

His mother, on the other hand, would not view this scenario as the potential end of the world. She would simply contact the bully's parents and notify the school authorities in order to get the problem resolved.

The child and the parent have two different percep-tions of the same problem.

Goals and Options

A goal is a dream with a deadline. I once heard motivational speaker Les Brown ask an audience the following question: "How do you eat an elephant?" His answer was, "One bite at a time." No problem is too large to tackle if we are willing to break it down.

Before you entered into your current relationship or marriage, you probably had an idea of how you wanted or expected things to be. It's time to take a look at where you stand in relation to your goal. Before you can live in black and white, you must first determine your wants and needs. It's important to differentiate your desires from those society states you should have. Not everyone wants a little house with a white picket fence and two and a half children. Not every woman wants a husband who is a business executive, physician, or attorney.

After you've done some introspective thinking, it is entirely possible you may come to the conclusion you already have everything you want in a mate. If you have determined your relationship has honesty, trust, loyalty, love and devotion, intimacy, and emotional security, then you are well on your way to having everything most couples wish for.

Making Lists

You can't see things in black and white until you write them down. I suggest you not use a computer or word processor to complete the following exercises. There is more of an emotional connection when something is written manually. Mind you, I have no scientific proof of this, but try typing up a new recipe containing six or more ingredients from a cook book in a computer document and then delete it. Now write down a completely different recipe with six or more ingredients on a piece of paper and throw it away. Wait an hour and see which recipe you recall best.

To begin this exercise, take one sheet of paper and write down everything you want in your ideal mate. Using another sheet of paper, draw a line down the center and place your mate's name on the top-left side of the paper. Now number the rows to correspond with the exact number of traits you listed on your initial "ideal mate" sheet of paper. For example, if you listed twenty traits you wanted in an ideal mate, and then number twenty rows on the sheet of paper you wrote your mate's name on.

Review your list of desired traits and write a Y for yes or N for no on the sheet containing your partner's name corresponding with the number of that particular trait. Take another sheet of paper and list all of the traits you wrote N next to. In the upper left-hand section, write the words "deal breaker."

Ask yourself the following question: If these traits never materialize, can I see myself staying in this relationship until I die?

Write the letter Y next to those traits you would love to have but could do without. Write the letter N next to those traits you consider a must-have. In reality, you have been doing without all of the missing traits thus far.

Count all of the traits on this sheet of paper that you have written the letter N next to. This is your number of deal breakers. Take another sheet of paper and list all of your deal breakers on it and set it aside.

Turn this sheet of paper over and draw a line down the center of the page. Write the word "Pros" on the left side and "Cons" on the right side. Quickly jot down the pros for staying in the relationship and the cons for leaving it. Beneath these, write the pros for leaving the relationship and the cons for staying.

Options

Keep in mind there are always options in dealing with your deal breaker list. Prior to making a final decision as to whether to stay in a relationship or leave, it is important to think about what happens *after* you make your decision. It's never wise to make a decision without seriously contemplating what is best for you in the long run. Whether you decide to stay or leave, you are bound to run into some challenges. Think of these challenges as the price of admission.

Only you can determine if you can afford a particular option at any given time. One very important factor is how much value you place on getting what you want. Usually the more we want something, the more we will are willing to pay. Payment need not be strictly financial. It can consist of time, mental energy, or physical energy. The most important aspect in making a decision about anything is to truly know *yourself*. Knowing your real needs and wants gives you clarity and purpose.

People who strive to lead a life in black and white tend to be proactive, decisive, and take action. People who live in a world of gray are likely to experience drama, uncertainty, and procrastination. They seek perfection in an imperfect world.

Life is short. Every decision you make is either bringing you closer to your goal or pushing you further away from it. The clock is ticking, and it's time you took control of your personal journey on earth. When we see things in black and white, we gain insight. When we see things in gray, it causes us to delay. Avoid the paralysis of perpetual analysis. Forgive yourself for any bad decisions you have made up to this point and strive to make better decisions going forward.

When We Change, Our Circumstances Change

Decision Time

The philosophy behind *My Cat Won't Bark!* is to first determine if the expectations you have of your mate are realistic based upon your knowledge of him or her. Let's review some of the central concepts of this book and determine what comes next in light of potential marriage plans.

As we've established, asking a liar not to lie, a thief not to steal, or a cheater to be loyal is the same as asking them not to be themselves! Those types of changes are internal personal decisions. They must be made by the individual. People change when they want to change.

You don't negotiate for love, and you can't manufacture chemistry. Remember real love, affection, and passion is given freely. It's futile to demand, coerce, plead, or force someone to give you what they don't have for you. Even if they try to change to please you, eventually they will revert back into their natural self. Apples never become bananas and cats never bark!

Communication is nothing more than sharing your thoughts, opinions, feelings, hopes, and desires with someone who is willing to listen and is intelligent enough to comprehend what you have stated. Not getting what you want does not mean there is a communication problem. Most likely you were heard and understood. In order to see changes from this person with regard to how they relate to you, they must still give a damn about you and the relationship. Without any emotional investment on their part, you may as well be talking to a wall.

Believe it or not, most of the time what we have to tell someone, be it praise or a complaint, is not a news flash to him or her. Often if it is something negative, they were probably trying to fly underneath the radar hoping you would not have the courage to bring up the issue.

There are only two possible reasons why your mate is not giving you what you want.

1. They don't have it to give.

2. They don't feel you are worth the effort to give it to.

After you have asked for what you want or need on several occasions in multiple ways, there comes a time when you have to take action. Ask yourself, "Is this a deal breaker?" If it is, then get out! If it's not learn to live without! If what you want is very important to you then you need to find someone who has what you want and is willing to give it to you.

On the other hand, should you decide to stay, you need to stop complaining and learn to appreciate the qualities your mate does have. As is often stated, "The definition of insanity is doing the same thing over and over again expecting a different result." If you want something different, you have to do something different. No amount of nagging, arguing, crying, or praying is going to change an apple into a banana. It is not your job to raise or train adults. Attempting to do so will lead to frustration, disappointment, and possible heartache. Peace will only come to you when you learn to either accept what you have or venture out to find what you need. There are two basic groups of people: those who get what they want and those who take what they can get. You have to know yourself. Following your natural instincts leads to happiness. A cat won't bark; it is not supposed to! Recognize what you do have and set your expectations accordingly. The following prayer has captured just that idea and is repeated regularly by people in difficult situations.

The Serenity Prayer

God grant me the serenity to accept the things I cannot change, courage to change the things I can, and wisdom to know the difference.

—Reinhold Niebuhr

Whenever you consider making a change in life, especially one that will affect another person, it's natural to question your loyalty and the true meaning of commitment.

Commitment: What Does It Really Mean?

Until Death Do Us Part?

Like a lot of things in life, commitment means different things to different people. Some believe it means once you make a decision, you stick with it no matter what you learn along the way. There are others who go to the other extreme by stating "I meant it when I said it."

A commitment is a pledge or agreement to dedicate one's efforts to insure a desired result.

Good Intentions

The majority of people on their wedding day have no thoughts of getting divorced or cheating. It's easy to be happy when the sun is shining and the sky is blue as they embark on a new adventure. In essence, on this day no one is lying about his or her intentions or desires.

Know Thyself Above All Else

One common mistake people make is signing onto something without knowing their tolerance for stress. Not everyone can withstand the same amount of pressures in life. This explains why a multimillionaire might commit suicide over a stock crash while someone barely existing in a third world country continues to forge on. Some people are clock watchers and can't wait to run out the door at 5:00 p.m. and others don't leave until the project they're working on is complete. Before giving your word to someone, it's important to know your vices and limitations. Biting off more than you can chew does not make you a bad person. It makes you an irresponsible person.

Due Diligence

The care a reasonable person exercises to avoid harm is part of the due diligence process. Basically, it's the process of uncovering important details *before* making a decision to move forward. In relationships we call this the dating or courtship phase.

Aside from spending time together and having fun, dating is a phase for gathering information and making observations in order to determine if a person is someone we want to have an exclusive relationship with or possibly marry. Does he or she want the same things as me? Do we agree on strategy as to the best way to reach our goals?

Making promises or commitments before you have important facts is a recipe for disappointment and failure. It takes more time to get to know someone than most people are willing to invest these days.

Beat the Clock

Another common mistake that leads to breaking promises or discovering one's inability to follow through on a commitment is having relationship goals tied to a specific time frame. For example: Within six months we should be saying "I love you" to each other. At the one year mark, we should be discussing our lives in terms of building a future together, which includes moving in together or getting engaged. Some couples literally go from the infatuation phase to becoming engaged without ever having a major disagreement!

They have no idea how their significant other handles stress. They don't know if the person they're seeing is living under a mountain of debt. Last but not least, they don't know if the person they are dating is being their authentic self or simply working hard to impress them in order to forge an emotional commitment.

Once the "save the date" notices are mailed, any doubts or trepidations are either dismissed or attributed to having cold feet. The couple's time is consumed with selecting venues, choosing flowers, picking the bridal party, and hiring the photographer, videographer, and DJ. They are also occupied with making honeymoon plans and attending the events such as the bridal showers and bachelor and bachelorette parties. The overwhelming nature of these preparations leaves no room for reevaluating the wisdom of the marriage itself.

Stick a Fork in It!

For many people, after the wedding day is a period where they relax. Vows have been exchanged, and at long last they have someone who is committed to spending the rest of their life with them. Mission accomplished.

Before marriage, many couples are very much like people rushing to catch an airplane; once aboard, they turn into passengers. They just sit there.

—Paul Getty

Getting Past New

Whether we want to admit it or not, most of us look forward to getting to a place or time where we can relax and take things for granted. We can't wait for the probation period to end at a new job. There is an element of stress that comes with trying to hold onto something. We look forward to a time where we don't have to put in our best efforts to maintain our position. In relationships, some people see this as the time where you don't have to worry about what you say or how you act because their significant other is *not going anywhere.* In their minds, "love and commitment" means "forever" *regardless* of what happens.

In reality there is no such place or time! Marriage, like a job, is an at-will contract. Being in a committed relationship does not mean you can stop being good to your mate and they won't go anywhere. No one is stuck with anyone. You have to keep impressing someone to keep them around.

Commitments Are Not Written in Stone

New information changes everything. If you agree to follow someone heading east to watch the sunset and along the way you discover their strategy is flawed, you are not under any obligation to keep going in the wrong direction just because you agreed to stick with them. Relationships are living, evolving things. Communication is your GPS navigational tool to keep track of where you are heading.

A commitment is only good for as long as both parties agree on a strategy to reach a desired goal. Being committed to someone does not mean you turn off your brain. You are still entitled to have deal breakers. In fact, if you don't have them, odds are you don't love yourself or you have low self-esteem.

If You Want **Something Different, You Have To Do Something Different**

Workbook Section - Finding Your Own Way

"At its fundamentally flawed core, the aim of almost any learning program is to help us become who we are *not*."
—Tom Rath, author of *Strengths Finder 2.0*

In this section, the goal is not to have you become someone different but rather to help you uncover who you are and determine exactly what it is you want. Having said that, there are times when it may be necessary to make adjustments in order to obtain the things you desire. If you want something different, you have to do something different.

Each person has to decide if making a change is essential to achieve happiness. The objective is to make decisions from a place of awareness. The better you know yourself, the easier it is to determine your needs and desires. I cannot stress this enough. The relationship you have with yourself is the most important relationship you will ever have. Once you know who you are and what you want out of life, the rest of your energy is used to chart your course and execute your plans. Life is a personal journey. Be true to yourself!

I think it's important we put another myth to rest before we get started. I'm sure you've heard people say, "You can't help who you fall in love with!"

My response is, "Really?"

I think it's a very romantic notion to believe we have no control over whom we fall in love with. However, in reality, we actually have to say yes an awful lot of times before we become an item with someone.

Yes! Yes! Yes!

First, there is a request to exchange contact information. Saying no here would stop things in their tracks. The next thing is agreeing to go out and spend some time together (another yes). This often leads to future dates. Eventually someone leans in for a kiss, which the other person accepts or turns away from.

Another date is proposed, and once again there is an opportunity to say yes or no. Someone makes a sexual move, which the other can either accept or reject. You are told things and you must decide to trust the person or not. Each and every time there was an opportunity to retreat by saying no or move forward by saying yes, the person that fell in love *chose* to say yes.

How Did This Happen To Me?

At any given point, saying no would have stopped a relationship from developing. It's amazing how people can say yes a hundred times, and when things go bad, they act as though things just happened or it was beyond their control. There is no escaping the fact *we choose our own friends, lovers, and spouses*. If you want an apple but buy an onion instead, whose fault is that? It's a waste of time and energy to curse the onion for not tasting like an apple.

We impulsively say yes to people who don't possess the traits we claim we want in a mate. There really is no point in creating a shopping list if you are going to ignore what is on it and instead purchase the candy bars, gum, chips, and National Inquirer when you get to the cashier. Every friend, lover, or spouse who has entered into your life is someone you consciously said yes to at some point. They didn't magically fall out of the sky and land into your life. There was no "It's bigger than the both of us" moment.

You made a choice, and if it turned out badly, assume responsibility and promise yourself to do better. You can help who you fall in love with by only dating those who fit your ideal criteria. Acknowledging choice is empowering!

Know Thyself

As I've stated multiple times, you have to know yourself and what you want and need from another person.

Hopefully with time and experience comes maturity and wisdom to help you stick to the items on your relationship shopping list and avoid making impulsive decisions. Never separate your mind from your heart when making relationship decisions. The purpose of the mind is to protect the heart!

How Do I Determine if My Mate Is My Ideal Partner?

If you want to try quantitatively assessing your compatibility, consider doing the following exercise.

Step One

List all of the traits you *want* in a mate.

Step Two

List all of the traits you *need* in a mate. These are your absolute must-haves.

Step Three

List the deal-breaker issues that would cause you to end or avoid a relationship.

Step Four

List the things you admire the most about your mate.

Step Five

List the things that bug you the most about your mate.

Step Six

Combine the number of "want" and "need" traits you desire in a mate.

Step Seven

Place a Y next to every trait you deem present and N for those that are missing.

Determine what percentage of your *wants and needs* traits are present in your mate and relationship. For example, let's say you have a total of twenty-five wants and needs traits with ten marked N. If you divide one hundred by your number of wants and needs, in this case twenty-five, you get four. This is your point value for each trait.

Subtract the ten N traits, which will leave you with fifteen Y traits.

Multiply your fifteen Y traits by your point value of four. Represented in equation form, $(15 \times 4) = 60$ percent.

59 percent and below is failing. You are either sleep-walking through the relationship or making plans to exit.

60 percent is borderline passing. You often imagine yourself being free of this relationship but lack the will to begin anew.

Disagreements are common.

70 percent is passing. Although far from perfect, you are committed and hoping for improvement as time marches on. You are open to counseling.

80 percent is good. It's not the dream relationship you imagined, but it is so much better than what most people have. You are grateful and would not risk trading places with anyone.

90 percent and higher is near perfection.

Congratulations—you have found your soul mate!

Step Eight

Throw the percentages out of the window! Relationships are not that easy to analyze. If they were, we could simply use mathematical calculations to find happiness. Let's face it: we don't value each and every single trait equally.

All Traits and Characteristics Are Not Equal!

Surly no one would consider a desire for breakfast in bed or special attention to be as important as having a partner who is devoted and sexually monogamous. And yet many self-help books subscribe to this use of mathematical formulas.

Only *you* can determine the value of each of the traits *you* desire. For some people, having sex, affection, and loving gestures from their mate is more important than having someone that earns lots of money. Another person may accept his or her mate's infidelity as long as the home and family needs are the top priority. This person requires that his or her mate's indiscretions remain discreet.

Many couples are content, dare I say happy, to simply be companions enjoying each other's company without sexual intimacy. Sexless marriages are more common than one would imagine. In many of these instances, couples are also sleeping in separate rooms.

As described in a previous chapter, intangibles such as *chemistry* play a major role in determining whom we end up having a relationship with. This explains why it is possible to meet someone who has every trait you say you want *on paper* and yet you don't click when you meet. It also explains why you sometimes impulsively jump into relationships with people whose traits if listed on paper would cause you to clutch your heart and run.

Our weakness prevails for reasons such as the person is very attractive, has a hilarious sense of humor, and is rich, powerful, exciting, or borderline dangerous. Often we think we are in control and believe we can indulge ourselves by having a short fling with these people for the thrill of it while passing time waiting for Mr. or Ms. Right to come along. However, flings have been known to drag into months or years, and in many cases can turn into ill-advised marriages. We get so caught up in the drama of trying to change water into wine because we've invested a large amount of time with the wrong person, and we miss Mr. or Ms. Right strolling by.

The only cure for impulsive relationships is time, bad experiences, and cultivating enough discipline to stick with your shopping list. A reasonably intelligent person learns to set aside their initial attraction to someone while taking the time to really get to know them as a potential spouse.

Familiarity Breeds Contempt

The very same traits that attracted you to your mate could also become the wedge in your relationship that drives you crazy. High intelligence becomes boring. Hot looks or sexiness becomes narcissistic or high maintenance. A great sense of humor is now seen as being silly or immature. Rich becomes materialistic and egocentric. Powerful become demanding and controlling. Exciting and spontaneous becomes manic, fickle, and unreliable.

A clear sign of maturity is when we learn to use our mind to protect our heart.

The following are tips for women but would work for men as well.

If you want to be married and your mate isn't interested, don't waste your time! Too many women believe that over time they can sell their man on marriage or having kids. They refuse to believe what he told them about the issue. Speaking as a man who also has male friends, I have never known any man to make up his mind to get married and set out *searching* for a wife. Most likely it begins with him looking at the woman he is with and asking himself, "Why not?" She's been with me a couple of years, knows my likes and dislikes, and takes care of me in various ways, and I can't imagine my life without her. I love her to death." Generally speaking, it is more of a discovery process and *not a goal* for most men. I once told everyone I met that I would never ever get married again! Marriage was definitely not one of my goals! But then I got married for the second time in August 2008.

Does the man you want to marry want you? Is he pursuing you? The man who is right for you *will* pursue you. If he wants to marry you, he will. Men are not indecisive about things *they want*. If a man believes you are worth the effort, he will make the effort. Kings have abdicated their thrones for women they fell in love with. Others have gone to war. If there is a guy who won't even pick up the phone to call you or does not show up as promised, it's plain and simple; as one former best-selling book states; "He's just not that into you." Far too many women try to rationalize why a man has not proposed to them. When a man, or anyone for that matter, truly wants something, they are not indecisive. Use what God gave you when searching for a mate: your brain.

What Makes You a Great Catch?

It's so easy to create a laundry list for others to live up to, but often we neglect to spend a single minute thinking about what *we* have to offer. Most people would rather be the buyer than the seller.

It's a good idea to take stock of ourselves before we create our shopping list. A broke person is not in a position acquire anything. You must offer value. But often it's the people with tons of baggage or the least to offer who are the ones demanding a Mr. or Ms. Perfect in return.

We have to grow into what we want. Like attracts like for long-term success in relationships, just like water seeks its own level.

As stated earlier in the book, I disagree with those who suggest marrying someone that loves you more than you love them. Eventually your spouse will come to realize that you are not putting 100 percent into the relationship, and they will either walk away or cheat on you. Or maybe you will end up cheating on them since you are not truly in love with them. It's impossible to fake passion or being in love forever. Simple romantic tasks that anyone in love looks forward to doing, you come to see as work. When someone realizes the person they would give their all to does not love him or her nearly as much, it's a heartbreaking day. That is the kind of heartache that no one deserves!

If you are *not truly in love* with a person, eventually you will find yourself becoming less affectionate with him or her, easily agitated, or exchanging harsh words without the use of a mental edit button because a part of you feels he or she is *lucky* to have you. Essentially you don't care about the other person's feelings or fear him or her leaving you. A small part of you may even feel relieved if your mate left because deep down you feel you settled for him or her. In this kind of a marriage, at times you will reminisce about someone *you actually were in love with* or passionate about, but you didn't stay with them because they were lacking in other areas. Marriages without passion are unhappy marriages without a doubt. Those who underestimate the importance of passion, intimacy, and romance in a marriage are often shocked by an affair. Ultimately, no one wants a beige marriage or one that simply looks good on paper. As I stated before, no one can fake a desire, need, or want forever.

One major difference in men and women is how they approach dating. Women are more practical than men. A very successful man would not think twice about dating a waitress who has no major goals if he considers her to be hot. Not many successful women would enter into a relationship with a waiter or busboy that has no major goals or aspirations. There is no such thing as a true male gold digger. If an unattractive, overweight woman was a multibillionaire, she would not have her pick of hand-some men everywhere she went because of her wealth. Now, if a short, fat, old, bald ugly man pulls up to a night-club driving a red Ferrari or exits a limo with bodyguards as he walks into the club, women who look like models will try to pursue him or welcome his advances.

If you are unhappy, does it mean there is something wrong with your mate? Not really. As long as they are honest about who they are and what they want, there is nothing wrong with them personally. They just may not be right for you! Here is my take: A man may be wrong for you and right for another woman! Just as you may be wrong for one type of man but right for another type of man! Values and priorities are different for everyone. When I say there is nothing wrong with any of us, what I mean is that just because we have not met the right person for ourselves does not mean there is something wrong with us. You are perfect for someone!

It is natural to feel there is something wrong with us when we don't have what we want. But we are simply going about things in a way that will not give us the results we want. For example: A man who wants to see lots of women meets a woman who wants to get married. Does either person have something wrong with them? My answer would be no. There is nothing wrong with either of them. They are just wrong for each other. In other words, they have different goals or needs. His lifestyle choice is no more wrong then her life style choice. They just have different wants. When he finds a woman that accepts his lifestyle, it will click for them.

When the marriage-minded woman meets a marriage-minded man, then things will click for them.

Ultimately we're all looking for someone who wants what we want.

It is connecting with someone who thinks and feels the way you do that makes them right for you. Everyone is right for someone. Your Mr. Right may be wrong for another woman but there is nothing actually wrong with him. When we meet someone who does not want what we want, we tend to judge them or say they have a problem or something is wrong with them. In reality, there is only agreement and disagreement. We are all looking for someone who *naturally agrees* with us on the major the things. We have a legitimate beef if this person presented himself or herself as wanting the same things we did but in fact could care less about our values. This would be lying or playing games. Now that is wrong!

Recently I posted the following article after hearing yet another woman ask the question:

Why Are There So Few Good Men?

Every now and then, I come across a television show in which a woman proclaims all of the good men are taken or all men are jerks! In reality there are probably just as many good men as there are good women.

Timing Is Everything!

A woman in her mid-twenties may be starting to think about marriage and family while her male counterpart is more interested in playing video games, getting high, drinking, and watching sports with his buddies. This same man most likely will have different priorities when he hits his mid-thirties. In essence, a twenty-five-year-old woman who is ready to get married and raise a family is better off dating a man who is closer to thirty-five. This is because women generally mature faster than men.

A woman in her twenties who insists on marrying a man her own age is often destined for disappointment. Life is too short to be wasting time trying to change water into wine! Trying to change your mate leads to frustration on your part and resentment on his or her part.

A "Bad Boy" Makes a Girl's Heart Beat Faster!

There are a lot of women who are more attracted to the bad boy, especially during their youth. Quite a few women will list all the wonderful traits they want in a man and yet they find themselves going after the complete opposite over and over again.

Selecting the wrong mate is the number-one cause of divorce. Hopefully, once a woman truly knows herself and what she wants, wisdom will kick in to help her become better at selecting people to become a part of her life.

The bad boy is a challenge, and he's exciting. His unreliability is seen as being unpredictable. Knowing that other women are pursuing him at the same time raises his stock. There is nothing like a little competition to make someone go all out to win. Chemistry and magnetism are stronger than logic!

There's a sense of emotional life–and–death drama always lurking beneath the surface. It's almost a cliché to hear a woman tell her friend, "I know he's probably up to no good, but there is something about that man I just can't get enough of!" One thing is for certain: Life with a bad boy is never boring!

Some women view the good guy as being too nice or weak, as someone they could run over; too predictable, safe, and *boring*. For many of these women, it is only after taking several trips on the roller coaster with the bad boy that they decide to settle down with a good guy. It's a practical decision and often has very little to do with chemistry. She treats the good guy differently than she did the bad boy.

The first night or soon after she met the bad boy, she had sex with him. She rode him like a horse in the Kentucky derby; they did everything sexually: oral, anal, spanking, and screaming. They took showers together, she sucked his toes, she gave him sensual massages, cooked breakfast and served it to him in bed, gave him her debit card and PIN, *loaned* him money and let him borrow her car, and so on. In return, all he did was sling some dick.

After she gets dumped or comes to realize she will never win over his heart, she sets her sights on finding a good guy, also known as Mr. Right. When this same woman meets a man whom she sees as good guy potential, you might think she would shower Mr. Right with all the love and affection she gave to the bad boy. Wrong! Now she breaks out Steve Harvey's ninety-day rule!

She's not going to have sex with Mr. Right until he commits to her emotionally and shows her he worships her, adores her, and would damn well die for her! When they finally do have sex, Mr. Right will *never* experience the same "freak between the sheets" sex action that was given to the bad boy. The risks for her are too high. If she takes him to the rodeo, she's afraid he may take her off his pedestal. In fact, a lot of women seem to believe that having sex too quickly with a man will *turn him into an a-hole*. If that's a woman's experience, she may want to have a doctor look her over. A jerk was a jerk before she had sex with him, just as sure as a true good guy on day one will still be a good guy in ninety days.

The lesson a lot of good guys get from watching this scenario over and over again is that bad boys have all of the fun and good guys get the leftovers. Hence the old saying, "Nice guys finish last."

Women Cope Better with Pain Than Men

If men bore children, there would be a lot of one-child families! This difference is true with emotional pain as well. Aside from watching the bad boy have all of the fun, a lot of former good guys who have gotten their hearts broken have never recovered. They never completely open up emotionally again. It takes more courage to fall in love a second or third time than it does the first time. Steven James Dixon discussed this in his self-published book titled *Men Don't Heal, We Ho—A Book about the Emotional Instability of Men*

Time Changes Everything

As the bad boy sheds his youth, he tends to behave more like a good guy. Some of it is due to maturity, and a lot of it is because he can't get away with what he used to anymore. "Every Saint has a past. Every Sinner has a future." Such is life.

Women become smarter about relationships as they age. They learn to let their feelings and their thoughts work together. There are good men all around if a woman is willing to open her eyes. They are not all over six feet tall, have an athletic build, with a head full of hair, possessing a dazzling smile, with dynamic personalities and earning over a hundred thousand dollars a year. There is the grocery store manager, the UPS driver, the mailman, the shoe salesman, the bus driver, the train engineer, the teacher, minister, computer programmer, taxi driver, butcher, and countless other men you pass by daily without giving a second glance who might offer all of *the important qualities* required to have a happy relationship: honesty, trust, loyalty, love and devotion, intimacy, and emotional security.

A lot of good guys are inclined to be more introverted, humble, down-to-earth, and less ego-driven. They don't make the same splashy entrance as the bad boy, but trust me, they are out there. They're everywhere. This universe is based upon balance. For every tune, there is a lyric waiting to be written. For every woman, there is a good man waiting to be found. Never give up!

Tips for Finding Your Mr. Right and Questions You Need Answered

This section is primarily geared toward female readers, but men may find these tips useful as well. The first activity will help you identify what you are looking for in a mate.

1. List all of the traits you want in a mate (e.g., education, social drinker, drug user, smoker, tall, short,

handsome, athletic, thin, overweight, income level, and attitude).

2. List the hobbies or activities your ideal mate would enjoy in his spare time.

3. Imagine the type of friends and acquaintances he would have.

4. What sort of goals would this person have? Is he civic-minded? A philanthropist?

5. Is he religious or Spiritual? An atheist? Does he believe in *The Secret*?

6. Is he more romantic than practical or vice versa?

7. Is he old-fashioned or progressive?

8. Is he an introvert or extrovert? Possess a love for the arts? An avid reader of books?

9. Has he been married? Does he want to get married? Or is he completely happy being uncommitted for the rest of his life?

10. Has kids/wants kids? Member of Parents without Partners? Never wants kids?

11. Is he the type of person who might register for an online dating service? If so, which ones would he consider? Which types would he avoid?

12. Make sure there are no conflicts in your desired traits.

Example: A CEO will not be home at 5:00 p.m. for dinner each night, and he may travel for weeks at a time. Therefore, if being together each evening is a priority for you, then this type of person is in conflict with your desires.

Use the Right Bait

One mistake women often make is they do not want to follow the hunter's basic rule: When you go hunting, bring the right bait! I hear women say, "I have a college degree, a great job, I own my home..." I tell them that's all great if you are looking for a w*oman*! Most men could care less if you are a waitress or a doctor! The majority of men are not looking to be taken care of. Your accomplishments are *the icing* on the cake. Men are attracted to a woman's physical attributes, personality, sense of humor and intelligence. *A hunter does not get to tell the prey what they should like or want.* She studies the creature's habits in order to attract him.

Reality Check Time

The Opposites Attract Myth: It's true, but not for the long haul! The truth is, people would rather be around people who have similar interests, goals, and attitudes toward life.

Take a Look in the Mirror: What do you bring to the table?

Write down all of your redeeming qualities.

Honestly, if you were the person you are seeking, would you want you?

Are you willing to actively and sincerely cultivate the traits you seek in someone else for life? (Not as a ploy.) If you want something different, you have to do something different.

Remember, the more attractive qualities a person has, the more competition there is to land him or her.

Love is like money: it's much easier to find than it is to hold onto. Once you have him, stay on top of things. Do not take your mate for granted. Love is like a garden that must be tended to because there will always be weeds and pests looking to attack your harvest. You are either nurturing or neglecting your relationship.

Transference: The art of becoming what you seek and looking outside of yourself.

Don't leave things to chance. Take control. The real secret to finding Mr. Right is you have to think like he would. In order to accomplish this, you must create a complete profile.

If you were Mr. Right, what type of job would you have?

What type of restaurants would you go to?

What would be your hobbies?

Would you belong to any specific organizations or clubs?

What type of music would you enjoy?

Would you join an online dating service? If so, which one?

Where would you go to meet women?

Are you a Republican or a Democrat?

Would you prefer to live in the city or in the suburbs?

Do you enjoy dancing?

Do you travel to exotic locations or prefer to stay within the United States?

What do you enjoy doing over the weekend?

Are you a sports fan? If so, which sporting events do you watch?

You want to live and breathe the same air he does or at the very least strive to do so.

You have to be where he is! Even if it's only in your imagination to begin with.

Once you become Mr. Right, you will know where to meet him.

Don't just visualize having this person in your life. You have to emotionally feel the feelings you would have if he were already in your life. Everything that you have began with a thought, a desire, a dream, or a visualization of it being yours. You imagined the *feeling* of having it before it was yours! If you were planning a vacation, you would visit various websites. You would look at photos and make a list of places you want to visit while there. You *anticipate* the trip with joy as the days roll by. You have already bought the ticket. There is no desperation or stressing over whether or not you are going. It's a done deal! This is how the law of attraction works! It's not just visualization, affirmations, and positive thinking. It takes believing so strongly that you *know* and *feel* it's on its way.

Once again, you must take action. Listen to your instincts and take cues that come from your subconscious. Understand it will take some time to reprogram yourself, but once you get there you will come to understand *believing is seeing*, not the other way around. It's been said, "Faith is to believe in what we cannot see and the reward of that faith is to see what we believe." Keep the faith!

Seeing, Believing, and Feeling

Whatever the mind of man can conceive and believe, it can achieve.
—Napoleon Hill

The above statement was made in a very popular book titled *Think and Grow Rich*. This book and many others, including *The Secret*, contain numerous examples of people reaching their goals by first visualizing or seeing, affirming, believing, and acting as though they have their goal *before it materialized* on the physical plane. Some people swear by the methods espoused in these books, and others see it as total hogwash. Just as some people believe taking vitamins daily is a way to remain healthy while others see it as simply manufacturing expensive urine.

If you desire to try some of the methods suggested in these works, the following is an example of how to apply one of them. Once again, I must stress there is more than one way to achieve any objective. In addition to mental preparation, one must also be willing to take action in accordance with suggestions provided by his or her instincts, hunches, or internal guide.

Find a place where you will not be disturbed. You may sit in a comfortable chair or lay flat on the bed or floor.

Begin by thinking about what it is you want and a scenario establishing proof of obtainment. Continuing with our earlier example of a woman in search of Mr. Right, she might imagine receiving a beautiful bouquet of roses while at work along with a card professing love. It is very important to establish a verification outcome that you may use to recognize your desire has been fulfilled just as you *imagined*.

Close your eyes and relax to a point where you feel drowsy. Imagine yourself sitting at your desk working. Your phone rings. It's the receptionist announcing there is delivery in the lobby for you.

Feel the joy of surprise in your heart; a smile slowly spreads across your face as you begin walking down the hall to the reception area. As you approach the lobby, you see one of the most beautiful rose bouquets.

The receptionist comments, "Somebody must really love you!"

You laugh as you walk away with the flowers in hand. Upon arriving at your desk you open the card. The inscription in the card almost moves you to tears. Allow yourself to soak up this feeling of joy as your heart says, "Thank you." Slowly open your eyes and go about the rest of your day. Repeat this daily.

Feel, act, and believe as though you know that what you desire will be yours!

A similar notion of having faith that your desire will come to pass is seen in the Bible. Matthew 9:27 says, "According to your faith it will be done for you."

In addition to using visualization, affirmations, and having faith, you also need to be alert.

Often the thing we want does not come about the way we expected it to.

You may be invited to a picnic or some other event out of the blue where you would normally decline, but something within causes you to give it a second thought. It is in these times where we must be able to determine if we are missing our opportunity to have what we want. The more in-tune we become with ourselves, the stronger our instincts become. Eventually we learn to trust our inner guide and follow its direction.

At some point we must take action to make our dream a reality.

People interested in starting relationships are using dating websites as one method of meeting other singles. One such site claims one in five couples getting married today met online. I imagine this percentage will rise in the future as more people become comfortable with the idea of online dating. There was a similar hesitancy in the past for many people when it came to using their credit card to make purchases online. Today, just about everyone I know of has purchased something online using a credit card.

One major cause of alarm for meeting someone online is trust issues. There have also been nightmare stories reported in the news concerning people who met online. Many of these stories are similar to the ones once reported during the days of disco and various other nightclubs. *Meeting strangers inherently contains risk.* The Internet is nothing more than a tool. It's neither good nor bad. Just as a fork can be used to eat a salad or a slice of double fudge cake, it's the person using it that determines whether they will have positive or negative results. The people online are the same people you would see at the grocery store, mall, beach, park, or church. *It's not where you meet but whom you meet that counts.* However, I would caution anyone to use common sense and be cautious when meeting strangers, regardless of how they come into your life.

Six Common Mistakes Women Make with Online Dating

Are you in search of love? Choose wisely.

Selecting Without Researching

Everyday there are lots of new dating websites popping up. One very common mistake people often make is assuming they are all about the same. Intellectually, you know that cannot be true. Would anyone compare staying at Motel 6 to staying at the Ritz Carlton or a Four Seasons Hotel by simply noting they all have beds and cable television? Do you believe a steak dinner at Denny's is just as good as one at Ruth's Chris Steak House? In a word, no!

And yet when it comes to online dating sites, lots of people don't exercise discriminating taste when making a selection. You owe it to yourself to at least do a few Internet searches to view the top-rated dating sites. Also, be aware there are sites that cater to particular interests. Before you sign up with any site, you have to ask yourself, if I were my Mr. Right, which online dating site would I choose?

Bad Profile Photo

Another big mistake is using a horrible profile photo. Examples include those who stand in front of a bathroom mirror holding a cell phone, pictures taken overhead with the subject looking up, photos holding a dog, cat, or some other pet, photos showing your ex's hand resting on your shoulder even though you have cropped his face out, glamour shots, photos with zany or stupid facial expressions, or those taken standing next to your best friend (who may be more attractive than you). A profile photo is your calling card, and the viewer's focus should be on you.

Lying

Lying about age, weight, career, and relationship status is a mistake. Eventually the truth comes out! Now, to be fair, some of these websites make it easy to be evasive with such options as "I'd rather not say," or "I'll tell you later." You can have a relationship status listed as "it's complicated" or a body type listing "a *few* pounds to lose." If one has to be discreet, he or she is involved with someone. Anyone with thirty pounds to lose is kidding herself by calling that a few". I'm certain if someone were hitting you on the head you would not consider 30 times to be a few.

Asking for the World!

"Don't expect to sit next to the moon unless you are a star!" Too many people are unrealistic when it comes to their search for a mate. They create a long list of requirements or traits that even they do not possess themselves. It is just as important to illustrate what makes *you* special. Like attracts like.

Others take the opposite approach by listing everything they do not want. (No players, no liars, no cheaters, no games, etc.) Without realizing it, they are announcing to the world this is who they have chosen in past relationships. It also comes across as if they are negative, bitter, or have a chip on their shoulder. Does anyone really believe a player who is attracted to you is not going to contact you simply because you said you do not want to deal with players? It should go without saying if a trait is not on your list of wants, then it is not something you desire. Focusing on the negative is never attractive.

Meeting Too Quickly

Another very common mistake is exchanging personal contact information and setting up dates too quickly. One of the great things about online dating sites is that you can get a feel for someone by how well they communicate with you through the site. You can use the online service's instant messaging to chat as well as e-mail one another through the site. If a man starts to rush you into meeting with him, more often than not it's because he is afraid he may expose some character flaw that might deter you.

Some women are afraid of becoming too emotionally invested with someone they have yet to meet. This forces them to hurry with exchanging contact information and meeting a guy too quickly. Hopefully you are communicating with multiple prospects and evaluating your options based upon the responses you get to questions you ask, their sense of humor, and things you have in common. You are responsible for your choices.

Pushing for Exclusive Status Too Quickly

Lots of women are in such a hurry to tie down a relationship with someone they barely know! The whole purpose of casual dating is to *determine* if this person is someone you want to have a serious or exclusive relationship with. Casual dating does not mean having sex with every person you have dinner with. It means taking things one step at a time and allowing them to unfold *naturally*. Dating is an exploratory process, so it's often counterproductive to say on your profile that you're looking for a serious relationship, a marriage-minded person, or a God-fearing man.

Attempting to jump into a one-on-one dating situation right off the bat is like job hunting by sending out one resume at a time and waiting to see if that company will interview you and eventually hire you before you send out a resume to a different company. Realistically, you can't determine if he is "the one" until after you get to know each other better, and that takes time. Be yourself and encourage him to do the same. No one goes to a buffet and stops only at the first station. The vast majority of people walk around and check out all the stations before deciding upon what they will eat. Every serious relationship I have ever had began casually and *evolved* into something serious.

It's also a mistake to automatically assume just because someone has gone out with you a couple of times they should take down their profile. Unless you have agreed to be exclusive, you both should keep your options open. Trying to skip the dating process in order to get married can lead to regret.

Dating is not a waste of time. Being married to the wrong person is.

Measure Twice and Cut Once

It's practically impossible to discuss dating without mentioning "the one" theory.

The One: Separating Myth from Reality

Seek and Ye Shall Find

Many of us believe there is only one special person out there that will get us. We'll share the same sense of humor, enjoy doing the same things, have the same goals, and be sexually compatible. In fact, many of us believe this person will instinctively know what it is we want or need without us having to ask or communicate our thoughts. We'll never have major disagreements and we'll live happily ever after. For many of us, our biggest fear is living a lifetime without ever finding our "one."

Numbers—One in Seven Billion

According to world population statistics, we just surpassed seven billion people inhabiting this planet. The sheer magnitude of this number would indicate there is at least one soul mate for everyone! So why is it so difficult to find "the one"?

Exclude versus Include

The concept of "the one" is based upon our natural tendency to exclude rather than include when it comes to finding love. For example, if a person states "the one" has to be a member of their own race, that automatically eliminates billions of people right there! If you went on to say he or she must have the same religious belief, that will cut down your options by several billions more. We narrow things further by stating "the one" must reside in our own country, state, or town. All of this is *before* we get to height, weight, age, occupation, education, hobbies, interest, goals, and so forth. Last but not least, our family and friends *must* also like him or her and vice versa! It is no wonder that by the time we get done *excluding* people, there is *only* one "right one" left!

Traits and Characteristics

I believe once we decide what is really important with regard to traits in a person we desire, we are likely to find "the one" sooner rather than later.

Each of us is looking for specific traits in another person. In addition to us believing they are "the one," it is necessary for them to believe we are "the one." Having mutual feelings is the challenge. Chemistry is also a requirement.

Let's assume you are looking for someone who has the following traits: a*ttractive, positive, affectionate, considerate, loving, healthy, romantic, passionate, great sense of humor, intelligent, enjoys traveling to exotic destinations, honest, trustworthy, loyal, dependable, financially secure and responsible.*

Surely out of seven billion people, there must be one person who fits this profile! The truth is, there are thousands if not millions or possibly billions of people who'd describe themselves as having all of these traits! Once again we ask, "Why is it so difficult to find 'the one'?"

Requirements Change Over Time

One of the reasons it is a challenge to find "the one" is because we look for different traits in a mate over the course of our lifetime. That perfect guy or girl at ages sixteen, eighteen, twenty-one, or thirty may not seem so ideal to us at ages thirty-five, forty, and beyond.

In fact, every new person we enter into a serious relationship with looks like "the one" until we realize they are not. The truth is, there are lots of "the ones" who have all of the traits you could want at any given time. As we mature, we become more realistic and practical. You come to realize there is no such thing as a "perfect person" for you. A three-hundred-pound woman or man is not likely to attract a Brad Pitt or Angelina Jolie type.

No one is going to be able to read your mind, complete your sentences, or fill your days with sunshine for eternity. You determine how large your pool of potential mates is going to be by your method of including or excluding. Naturally, the fewer options you have, the more difficult it becomes to find a suitable mate. One must be willing to put him or herself in places and situations where they are likely to meet the type of person they want to attract.

Right and Wrong

The type of person that may be "right" for you may be "wrong" for someone else. When it's all said and done, there really is no "right" or "wrong" in relationships. There is only agree and disagree. Ultimately, we are all looking for someone who *naturally agrees* with us on the major things in life!

Love isn't finding the perfect person. It's seeing the imperfect person perfectly.
—Sam Keen

What Makes a Woman Good in Bed?

Too much of a good thing is wonderful.
—Mae West

Recently I was asked what makes a woman good in bed. Like most things in the area of attraction and pleasure, the answer will vary from man to man. Whenever I've read articles dealing with what makes a man good in bed, they normally start off with how he touches the woman, being gentle, kissing, foreplay, and his ability to hold back until she is ready to climax. Certainly all of the above are important, however, I believe it's possible for two men to touch a woman, kiss, and fondle her in the exact same ways and yet she will have a different reaction to each. The reason for this is that sex is said to be 75 to 80 percent mental.

How a person feels about someone, the chemistry they have with them, and physical attraction all come into play. This is especially true for couples in serious relationships. Nonetheless, there are instances where one can have mind-blowing sex with someone they just met. Sometimes it can be attributed to pure animal magnetism, and other times it simply comes down to the mood the woman is in. Perhaps it's been so long since she had sex that the slightest touch would lead her to explode.

When it comes to men, there are slightly different things that place one woman above another woman. Please keep in mind there is no one answer, and men vary just as much as women. Therefore, the following is in general terms and mixed with my opinion. I don't profess to speak for all men!

She Loves Sex

Anyone who loves what they are doing is usually good at it! They are always keeping an eye out for new and different ways to rock their mate's world as well as enhance their own experience. This may entail reading books such as *Tickle His Pickle*, watching adult films to steal techniques, or simply having discussions with close girlfriends to get tips. Simply put, *they want to be the best* and take pride in being skillful.

She Is Proactive in Reaching Her Own Orgasm

The number-one thing that makes a woman memorable to a man is when he knows he blew her mind in bed. I'm not talking about embracing the art of faking orgasms. Essentially, this goes back to her loving sex. It's difficult to love something without getting enjoyment out of it. A woman who has *explored her own body* and knows how to bring herself to climax can pretty much guide any man that is not naturally instinctive in the ways of pleasing her.

"You can't teach what you don't know!"

A sexually proactive woman doesn't simply lay back and leave things up to chance. She will shift her body, get on top, and even manually stimulate herself during intercourse if the position they are in allows for it. This woman knows her man is going to keep thrusting until he climaxes, and she is willing to do her part to make sure that she climaxes as well. His body is her tool, and she knows just how to use it to get the results she wants.

Men are turned off by overly passive women who lie on their backs and expect him to "Make the magic happen." Great sex is not for the timid! There are many women who mistakenly believe the reason a man stopped calling is because "he got what he wanted." However, in many instances, it is just the opposite. The sex was boring! Nobody wants boring vanilla sex! A proactive woman takes matters in her own hands or mouth to get the ball rolling if necessary. The number-one complaint most men have regarding bad sex with women is that they didn't move, coupled with an overall lack of passion and silence.

She Is Vocal

Sex in silence is a real buzz kill! The only exception is if you're being quiet to keep from being discovered. In this case it can be intensifying as you force yourselves to hold back your noises. However, for the most part, sex without any moans, rapid breathing, screams of passion, body-clutching tension, or naughty four-letter words can seem like taking a walk around the block. Even if you are not a moaner or screamer, words of encouragement can enhance a session. "That's it!" "Keep it right there!" "Don't Stop!" "Yes! Yes! Yes!"

Hell, most guys would settle for having a woman pound the mattress, squeeze a pillow, or mumble inaudible sounds while turning her head from side to side. Once again, this is not about acting or faking orgasms. It's about being vocally expressive when things do feel good.

She Flirts and Uses Sexual Innuendo

Men love to feel desired too!

A woman who expresses she has sex on her mind during the course of the day is a real turn on. This can be done with a naughty voicemail or e-mail indicating what she wants to do with him or reflecting back on something they have done the night before or at a prior time.

Some women give their partner's penis a pet name which can be used in code during a conversation along with a pet name for her vagina. It can be as spicy as you want it to be or as tame as "Tell Johnny Tammy says hello."

The point is, she lets her man know she is thinking of him in sexual terms and he is desired. A man in love will work hard to continue getting that type of response from his woman.

She Surprises Him

A woman who has a knack for doing the unexpected from time to time will easily separate herself from other women. Naturally, it helps to know how open-minded her man is. This could range from wearing something sexy or nothing at all when he gets home, to bringing toys, chocolate syrup, crushed ice, heat sensation lotions, jells, and adult board games to bed. Or it could mean jumping in the shower to play in the suds or giving him unexpected oral pleasure while he's watching television or doing some mundane task. Booking a room at a romantic-themed hotel, such as Sybaris or Essence Suites can make for quite a memorable time.

Practice Makes Perfect

Whether you are a woman or a man, the only way to become good or great at anything is to have the intention of being so. In the long run, no one is great at anything by accident. It all starts with having the desire and the willingness to put in the effort. Naturally, with each new relationship one becomes involved in, the first few sessions will entail going through your standard go-to moves based upon your past experiences.

No two people are the same. However, in a long-term relationship or marriage, one is presented with an opportunity to refine his or her skills to their specific mate. Given time, you can learn what every sigh or body movement means, guiding you toward your next move of deciding whether to tease or to please. Communicating desires and fantasies outside of the bedroom is just as important as giving queues inside the bedroom.

"Monogamy becomes boring when couples become lazy"

Law of Reciprocity

You will know you have found your sexual soul mate when they demonstrate the need to please you as much as you make the effort to please them.

The Way We Were

It's extremely difficult to let go of a great sex partner even if you know they are not right for you in many other ways. Most of us have experienced at one time or another being involved with someone who was absolutely incredible in bed but we had sense enough to move on for various other reasons. Unfortunately, the memories of being with them linger in our minds and haunt us from time to time. For whatever reason, you may not end up in a fairy tale relationship with the person you are presently seeing, but you can live on forever in his or her mind. A great lover is impossible to forget.

To live in hearts we leave behind is not to die.

——Thomas Campbell

One Man's Opinion!

Sometimes it helps to think about our relationships within the context of life as a whole. The following is an article I wrote on life and living.

News Flash! We're All Going To Die!

Making It Count!

Several years ago I was watching an episode of *Six Feet Under* on HBO. In this particular episode, there was a woman grieving over the loss of her mother. At one point she asked the funeral director, "Why do we have to die?"

He took a moment and then he said, "To make life important."

Whenever there is an unlimited supply of anything, we tend to value it less. A person in his or her early twenties may view a life span of eighty years as an eternity. Playwright George Bernard Shaw's saying that "Youth is wasted on the young" seems to apply here.

The Most Precious Commodity

Time is the most precious commodity on earth. We don't know how much of it we have, and yet many of us live our lives as though we have a thousand years left to go. The clock is always ticking. In the back of our minds we know we are going to die, but we continue to procrastinate doing things we say we want to do. We are all believers in the "Church of Tomorrow." But time is the one thing you can't recover. When a second, minute, hour, day, week, month, or year passes by, it's gone forever.

Midlife Crisis or Midlife Awakening?

There comes a point in everyone's life where they realize time is running out. This awareness of a finite number of years may begin to sink in at age thirty-five, forty-five, or fifty-five. Our trigger points vary. For some of us, it begins when more and more people in our age group start to die, such as high school and college friends, siblings, or co-workers. Another person may get a reality check when his or her new boss is ten or more years younger than him or her. It sends a subliminal message indicating they have climbed as high on the corporate ladder as they are likely to.

Some observe the difference in how other people treat them. A woman may notice that men aren't eyeing her as much as they used to and younger women refer to her as "ma'am." A man may pay a young woman a compliment and her facial expression screams "dirty old man!" or he's having lunch with a male co-worker and the waitress asks if the co-worker is his son. The AARP mails them monthly newsletters with invitations to become a member. The empty nest may serve as a trigger for others.

No matter who you are, at some point you become aware you have more years behind you than ahead of you.

A large segment of the population refers to this period as a midlife crisis, but I tend to see it as being more of a midlife awakening. Either way you look at it, the train has left the station, and it's up to you to decide how you want to complete your journey.

Today Is Tomorrow

The best way to make the most of each day is to act as though there is no tomorrow. Understandably, this is not always practical; however, the purpose behind this approach to life is to get you moving. Stop wasting time!

Bucket Lists

Keenly aware that we don't have an infinite number of years on the planet, it is up to each and every one of us to decide upon the things we would like to see, do, or accomplish before our final sunset. Life is a personal journey, and no one can decide what is important to you.

Make a list of things you want to experience, places you want to visit, and things you want to learn. Plans, dreams, and goals give us something to live for and strive toward.

A Life Without Dreams Isn't Living, Only Existing

Some of your goals will be easy to accomplish; others may require extreme creativity, and still others may not become a reality before your time here is done. It's been said, "It is not the destination but the journey that gives life its meaning."

Whether you are a billionaire or don't make enough to afford a home, in the end we are all going to die. You may as well try and swing for the fences while you're up at bat. Let us be remembered for how we *lived*!

Always remember, the world may not owe you anything, but you owe yourself the world!

Parting Thoughts

In closing, I'd like to thank you for taking the time to examine the choices you have made up until now. Making changes in one's life is not always easy, and the older we become, the more we think of the word *change* as being another word for risk.

There are two basics groups of people: those who get what they want and those who take what they can get. Being true to yourself is what leads to happiness.

Whether you decide to stay the course or set sail towards the open sea to fulfill your dreams, keep in mind that life is a personal journey.

Only you can determine what is right for you!

Know **Yourself,**
Love Yourself, and
Trust **Yourself**

Memorable Sayings and Ideas

If you want to remind yourself of the major concepts we've covered in this book, I've listed them all here as a convenient reference.

Life is a personal journey.

When we change, our circumstances change.

The only person you can control is yourself.

People change when *they* want to change.

You are responsible for your *own* happiness!

Your life is the result of the choices and decisions you have made.

If it's a deal breaker, get out!

If it's not a deal breaker, learn to live without!

Don't expect to sit next to the moon unless *you* are a star!

It's easier to maintain a fire than it is to reignite a spark.

You don't negotiate for love and affection. These things are given freely.

You don't manufacture chemistry. It's either there or it's not.

You are either growing together or growing apart.

There is no neutral; you are either nurturing or neglecting your relationship.

Communication is not an "Ask and it shall be given" proposition.

Don't assume communication will lead to action.

The one rule in love is there are no rules!

If commitment meant forever, there would be no such thing as divorce.

A marriage based upon circumstances rather than love is likely to fail.

Staying together for the sake of staying together is not a recipe for happiness; it's a design for building a prison.

It takes courage to look at the truth of a situation and make a change.

It takes patience and tolerance to accept people as they are.

Walking on eggshells can lead to having a nervous breakdown.

When we see things in black and white, we gain insight.

When we see things in gray, it causes us to delay.

It's not where you meet; it's whom you meet that counts.

Communication is always better than assumption.

If someone believes you are worth the effort, they will make the effort.

Never separate your mind from your heart when making relationship decisions.

Trusting someone does not mean you can't ask questions. Trusting someone means you believe they will give you *honest* answers to your questions!

Be yourself and let the chips fall where they may.

Know yourself, love yourself, and trust yourself.

Ultimately we are all looking for someone who *naturally agrees* with us, loves us, and accepts us as we are.

A life without dreams isn't living; Only existing.

It's been said men fall in love with their eyes and women fall in love with their ears. However, with age comes wisdom. Men learn all that glitters is not gold, and women learn actions speak louder than words.

There is no amount of *communication* or *work* that can overcome being with someone who does not want what you want.

The most important relationship you will ever have is the one with yourself.

It's your life. Take the wheel!

The world may not owe you anything, but you owe yourself the world!

CPSIA information can be obtained at www.ICGtesting.com
Printed in the USA
LVOW071541110113

315395LV00012B/603/P